ADDISON WESLEY LONGMAN HISTORY IN DEPTH SERIES

THE ORIGINS OF THE FIRST WORLD WAR

STUDY CENTRE

book is due return on or before th

...aham Darby
Series editor: Christopher Culpin

CONTENTS

PART ONE

INTRODUCTION

Causation: the long and the short of it

Because the First World War lasted so long and proved to be so bloody, historians used to assume that so momentous an event must have had numerous long-term causes. It was unthinkable that something so violent, that resulted in the deaths of anywhere between 10 and 25 million people, could have happened almost by accident or as a result of events that seem to be, with hindsight, quite trivial. Accordingly, historians have started their books on the causes of the First World War as far back as 1871, or 1878, or 1890 or 1894, looking for events that led up to the catastrophe of 1914 and after – and this book is no exception.

But we know from experience in our own time with events such as the collapse of the Soviet Union, the Iraqi invasion of Kuwait or the fall of Margaret Thatcher, that though these events may well have had long-term causes, when they occurred they came as a complete surprise to contemporaries. We should always be aware that nothing is inevitable in history (otherwise we would be able to predict the future) and that last-minute changes in events can lead to a completely different outcome. Perhaps the First World War would not have happened if Archduke Franz Ferdinand's driver had not taken a wrong turning in Sarajevo.

Of course all events that precede a single event are its causes, but it is the duty of the historian and the student to distinguish the important from the unimportant and to establish a hierarchy. It is also their duty to identify the relative merits of long-term and short-term causes and try to make a satisfactory distinction between them. It seems to me that short-term causes are paramount because without them long-term causes would not exist as the causes of anything at all. In some cases long-term causes are often the invention of hindsight – because we know an event took place, we look further and further back for the reason for its occurrence, ignoring perhaps the more decisive short-term factors. It is important to remember that the decision-makers of 1914 had no idea that they were embarking on over four years of carnage. Most people felt the war would be short – 'over by Christmas', as many put it. Many may have felt it would be confined to the Balkans (see Figure 2 on page 26). Seen in this light it is conceivable that the decisions to go to war might have been made at the last moment and were not long planned (despite the fact that the Schlieffen Plan had been drawn up 20 years before).

Another problem with long-term causes is that we also have to consider why events did not occur before they did (the subject of Chapter 2). Thus for some time before 1914 we see that rival alliance systems, imperial rivalry, the arms race, mutual suspicion and so on all existed – at the time of the Moroccan crisis of 1905–6, the Bosnian crisis of 1908–9 and the second Moroccan crisis of 1911 – without causing a war; therefore there had to be something rather special about 1914.

Now this is not to say that the long-term situation should be ignored – far from it (Chapter 1 takes us back to 1871). The long-term situation defines and delimits the context in which events occur. Moreover, it is the duty of the historian to reveal those long-term factors that were hidden from contemporaries. Also, long-term factors often come into play once a war has begun – they account for how events unfold and they often have to find resolution. This is how confusion can sometimes arise; a long-term factor can affect the course of events after a given point without being a cause of how events came to that point.

This book will look at the long term as well as the short term. It will hopefully help you decide what to put in, and what to leave out. After all, it is one of the major problems with this topic – how far should you go back? Where do you start? 1871, 1878, 1890, 1894, 1905, 1907, 1912 or 1914? It is often the case that the student or historian has to deal with the long-term factors if only to dismiss them as not directly relevant. Even if it is decided that the last six weeks are the most crucial, what came before is still important. For instance, the Kaiser's difficult birth in 1859 may have had a decisive effect on the events of those July days of 1914.

As you go through this chapter, think about the following questions:

◢ **What constitutes major power status?**

◢ **What were the relative strengths and weaknesses of the powers?**

◢ **Which of these powers constituted the greater threat to peace, and why?**

Political and diplomatic events

1871	Unification of Germany
1879	Dual Alliance between Germany and Austria
1890	Bismarck resigns
1892–4	Franco–Russian Alliance
1904	*Entente Cordiale* between Britain and France Russo–Japanese War (to 1905)
1905	First Moroccan crisis
1906–12	Anglo–German naval race
1907	Triple *Entente* – Britain makes agreement with Russia
1908/9	Bosnian crisis
1911	Second Moroccan crisis
1912–13	The Balkan Wars – Serbia doubles in size
1914	Assassination in Sarajevo (28 June) Austria declares war on Serbia (28 July) Germany declares war on Russia (1 August) Germany declares war on France (3 August) Britain declares war on Germany (4 August) Austria declares war on Russia (6 August) Failure of Schlieffen-Moltke Plan (September) Turkey joins war on German side (November)
1915	Italy joins war on *Entente* side
1917	Russian Revolution(s). Tsar Nicholas abdicates USA declares war on Germany
1918	Russia pulls out of war (March) German offensive fails (by the summer) Austria and Turkey collapse (October) Germany surrenders (November)
1919	Treaty of Versailles (June): Article 231, War Guilt Clause, blames Germany for the war

An introduction to the Great Powers of Europe in 1914

	Britain	France	Russia	Germany	Austria-Hungary
Population	46.4 m	39.6 m	167 m	65 m	49.8 m
Soldiers after mobilisation	711,000[1]	3.5 m+	4.4 m[2]	8.5 m[3]	3 m
Merchant fleet (tonnes)	11.7 m	1.1 m	0.4 m	3.1 m	0.5 m
Battleships	64	28	16	40	16
Cruisers	121	34	14	57	12
Submarines	64	73	29	23	6
Annual value of foreign trade	£1,223 m	£424 m	£190 m	£1,030 m	£198 m
Annual steel production (tonnes)	7 m	4.3 m	4.4 m	17.3 m	2.6 m
Railway (kilometres)	37,723	40,990	74,949	63,469	44,328

[1] Throughout the empire
[2] 5.9 million planned
[3] Theoretical maximum; 4.15 million immediately

Germany

What is truly remarkable about Germany is that it went from being a cluster of insignificant states in the 1850s to the most powerful state in Europe, in the period of a lifetime. Before 1871 the geographical area known as Germany had consisted of 39 states of varying sizes. Thirty-eight of these had been brought together in a process known as unification. In reality, this meant their conquest by the largest state, Prussia, in a very short space of time. Under the guidance of Otto von Bismarck, Prussia's first minister, the northern protestant states were absorbed in 1866 and the southern catholic ones in 1871. The new state was known as the Second Reich (Empire) and the Emperor (Kaiser) was the King of Prussia. The Empire had both a central government and a *federal* structure. Its political structure was authoritarian and conservative though there was a parliament (the Reichstag – elected by universal suffrage) with little power. Germany, then, was a new nation, but it developed quickly.

KEY TERM

Federal – a system in which states unite under a central authority but are independent in internal affairs.

The sheer speed and extent of Germany's growth in industrial, commercial and military/naval terms was phenomenal and by 1914 had put it well ahead of France and Russia, and probably Great Britain as well. Germany had a relatively well-educated population, an efficient army, a protected and productive agricultural sector and prodigious industrial growth. Coal production was second to Great Britain but steel production exceeded that of Britain, France and Russia combined. Exports tripled between 1890 and 1913 and it would only be a matter of time before the country would overtake Britain as the world's leading exporter. The dramatic build up of the German navy under Alfred von Tirpitz (to second in the world behind Britain in a decade) was another impressive indication of German capacity.

Interestingly, for political reasons the German army was not expanded so dramatically (the *elite* feared socialist infiltration of the ranks and a dilution of the social standing of the officer corps), but between 1910 and 1914 there was a change of gear as expenditure doubled. Furthermore, Germany could mobilise and equip millions of reserves, and the army's equipment and training was of the highest standard.

KEY TERM

The **elite** is an exclusive group of people; in the case of Germany the military and landowning aristocracy.

What were Germany's weak points? The answer: its geography, its political structure and its diplomacy. The creation of such a powerful new state in the middle of Europe perturbed all its neighbours. Moreover, it had little room for expansion either in Europe or overseas. When Foreign Minister von Bülow declared in 1899 'the world is already partitioned', he was expressing a resentment widely held in Germany. Germany was a great power but had missed out on the imperial pickings. (According to Bismarck, the Great Powers were Britain, France, Austria, Russia and Germany. The United States was seen as geographically remote and Italy was not considered to be of the first rank.) Under Bismarck, suspicions were allayed as he provided the Second Reich with cautious statecraft, but under Kaiser Wilhelm II (1888–1918) suspicions were aroused. Policy was chaotic – partly due to the monarch's personality flaws and partly due to the absence of collective responsibility and decision-making in government. The result was a restless and incoherent diplomacy which succeeded in alienating everyone. As Bethmann Hollweg, the Chancellor, put it in 1914, the result of German diplomacy was 'to challenge everybody, get in everyone's way and actually, in the course of this, weaken nobody'. Germany then, was a threat to the balance of power. Moreover, social tensions were growing too as the conservative landowning and military aristocracy sought to maintain its privileged position in the face of the growing aspirations of the increasingly articulate and prosperous middle and working classes. Germany was a strange mixture of medieval and modern – a technologically advanced state ruled by *divine-right monarchy*.

KEY TERM

Divine-right monarchy is a system of rule by one person, a king, who is believed to be God's appointed representative on earth and that as such the king is answerable only to God.

Austria-Hungary

The Habsburg family had ruled Austria since the thirteenth century and the Austrian Empire had emerged from the Napoleonic Wars intact and indeed enhanced with considerable influence over the German Confederation (it was one of the 39 states) and the Italian peninsula (ruling directly over Lombardy and Venetia). However, Austria's failure to take sides in the Crimean War (1853–6) led to its isolation and this in turn brought about its expulsion from both Italy and Germany, in unsuccessful wars against France in 1859 and Prussia in 1866. In the aftermath, recognition (and self-government) was given to Hungary by the establishment of the Dual Monarchy in 1867.

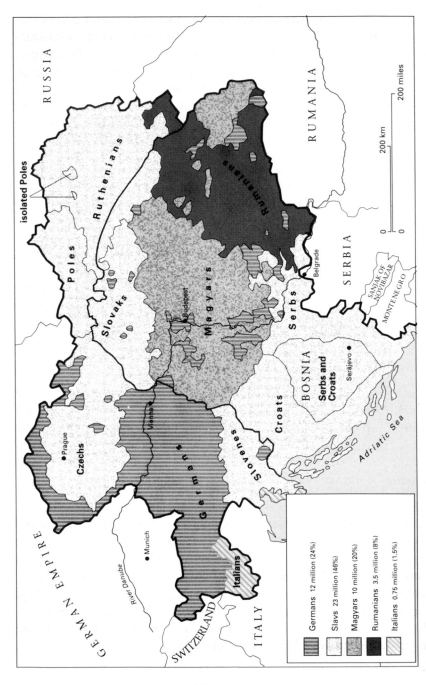

Figure 1 The linguistic and ethnic divisions of the Austrian Empire

Germans 12 million (24%)

Slavs 23 million (46%)

Magyars 10 million (20%)

Rumanians 3.5 million (8%)

Italians 0.75 million (1.5%)

One of the main characteristics of the Empire was its ethnic diversity as Figure 1 indicates; it consisted of 11 nationalities speaking 15 different languages. Over time the monarchy had spread out from Austria into Bohemia, Slovakia, Hungary, Ruthenia, Poland, Rumania, Slovenia, Croatia and so on. After 1867 the main focus of Austrian attention was the Balkans and the problem of the South Slavs. In terms of ethnic composition only 24 per cent of the Empire were Germans, 29 per cent Magyars (Hungarians), but a considerable 46 per cent were Slavs.

Austria-Hungary was in fact the least of the five Great Powers but its population was ahead of Britain and France and its industrial capacity in certain areas was reasonably good. However, there were enormous regional differences which largely mirrored the ethnic differences. Industry was taking off in the Austrian and Czech provinces, and agriculture was improving in Hungary, but in the other Slavic regions there was poverty, made worse by an accelerating rate of population growth. The relationship between Austria and Hungary was strained, but the largest danger to the unity of the Empire came from the Balkan nationalism of the South Slavs. Although the army was a unifying institution there was little money available for it as the government had to pay well over three million civil servants to hold the Empire together. The Habsburg Empire was militarily weak – and yet it had a number of potential enemies, such as Italy, Rumania and Serbia, not to mention Russia. Clearly, Austria could not fight on all these fronts. It needed German support; it could do nothing without it. Politically, the Empire was a conservative (German) autocracy; as with Germany, decision-making was in the hands of only a few. The final word rested with the Emperor, Franz Josef (1848–1916).

France

France had recovered from the Napoleonic Wars and had enjoyed something of a revival of its great power status during the Second Empire (1852–70). However, Napoleon III's defeat at the hands of Bismarck and the Prussians, and the loss of Alsace-Lorraine, had led to the formation of the Third Republic, which for many years was kept isolated by Bismarck's statecraft. However, by 1914 France had friends (Russia and Britain) and, unlike Austria, only one enemy, the German Empire (differences with Italy had been resolved).

France also had a huge overseas empire, principally in Africa and the Far East, which was second only to that of Great Britain, though its commerce was not substantial. Politically, the Third Republic was unstable with frequently changing governments that gave little continuity to military and naval affairs. The navy was no match for that of the British (and later the Germans) and the republican politicians put little faith in the army's loyalty (the **Dreyfus case** was only one manifestation of this problem). In fact it was not until after 1911, in the face of the growing German threat, that the army was properly reorganised.

KEY TERM

The **Dreyfus case** was where Dreyfus, a Jewish French officer, was unjustly accused in 1893–4 of delivering secrets to Germany. He was court-martialled and transported to Devil's Island. The subsequent outcry led by the novelist Zola (1898) led to a pardon (1899) but there was no full exoneration until 1906. The case highlighted the vehement antisemitism among right wing circles in the army, and the split between right and left in the Third Republic.

The state of the French economy is more difficult to get to grips with. Given the small increase in the French population in these years, measurements of growth and exports calculated on a per capita basis are impressive, but in comparative terms France was not doing well. It did have considerable mobile capital (second only to Britain) and invested heavily in Italy, Turkey, the Balkans and above all Russia, but in terms of industrial output and exports, it was lagging behind. France had not been able to keep up with Britain, and now it was dwarfed by the Germans whose steel and coal production was six and seven times as much, respectively. France remained highly agricultural (40 per cent of the workforce in 1910) and the Méline Tariff of 1892 simply supported inefficient farmers. By 1914 France's national income was half that of Germany's. And whereas Germany's population grew by 18 million between 1890 and 1914, France's only went up by one million. The lesson was obvious: despite impressive conscription rates, if it came to another war like 1870–71, the Germans would win again. However, the real lesson was to avoid a one-on-one struggle – and here French diplomacy proved to be its salvation, obtaining an alliance with Russia, improved relations with Italy and an entente with Great Britain.

Economically, France might have been no match for Germany in 1914, but psychologically it was. France was a confident nation in 1914.

Great Britain

Great Britain looked very impressive on paper, possessing the largest empire the world had ever seen, containing a quarter of the planet's population. Britain had the largest navy, the largest merchant marine; it was the biggest trader, investor, banker, insurer ... Yet the tide was turning against it. For a long time after 1815 Britain's maritime and industrial pre-eminence had been unchallenged; however, after 1870 the spread of industrialisation in Europe and the United States and its effects on military capacity eroded Britain's position. The rise of the United States of America, the expansion of Russia, the scramble for Africa, the penetration of China, all served to diminish British power and influence. Now that there were challenges everywhere, Britain by the 1890s found itself overstretched. It simply could not be strong in so many different places at one time.

Perhaps more serious was the erosion of Britain's industrial and commercial pre-eminence. Industrial growth fell, markets were lost and imports increased. Manufacturing output fell from a 23 per cent world share in 1880 to 13 per cent in 1913 – similarly, the share of world trade fell from 23 per cent to 14 per cent in the same period. Overall, the United States and Germany moved ahead. All this relative decline engendered quite a bit of pessimism as the twentieth century dawned. However, being number three in the world still made Britain a great power and it possessed immense wealth – enough to fight a modern, industrialised war. Also, the insularity of the British Isles (as opposed to the people!) freed the population from the fear of sudden invasion. Britain possessed so much territory that it was able to make a compromise here and there to avoid conflict – a factor that perhaps gave it more faith in diplomacy than might have been justified. Britain was still a major player, but could no longer afford to go it alone. It needed friends, but it also needed the flexibility to avoid commitments. This made it very difficult for decision-makers in Paris and Berlin to anticipate Britain's future policy.

It is interesting to note that when war was imminent at the end of July 1914, no one quite knew what Britain would do. Moreover, because

Britain had a well-established parliamentary system (which was by degrees democratised during the nineteenth century), the decision-makers in the British government did not always know what they could do. They had to be more solicitous of the views of others – MPs, press and public opinion – certainly more so than their counterparts in Berlin and Vienna.

Russia

Russia emerged victorious from the Napoleonic Wars in 1815 as one of the major powers; however, defeat in the Crimean War (1853–6) was a shattering blow. The defeat revealed Russian backwardness and inspired Tsar Alexander II (1855–81) to initiate a series of reforms designed to modernise (but not liberalise) the world's largest country.

By 1914 Russia possessed the largest peacetime standing army and its military expenditure exceeded that of Germany. Railway building went on apace and a new fleet was being constructed. The growth of Russian power caused grave concern to governments in both London and Berlin. Was this concern justified? It is difficult to assess, since Russia was both powerful and weak at the same time. Since the Crimean War Russia had industrialised and the annual growth in output was impressive. The production of coal, oil, textiles and steel grew rapidly. In many areas Russia had overtaken Austria and France and in the two decades before 1914 foreign trade tripled. A combination of foreign and state investment had turned Russia into the fourth largest industrial power in the world.

However, the other side of the coin is the fact that Russia's was not a mature economy. It was 'labour-rich but technology-poor' and was devoted to textiles and food processing rather than engineering or chemicals. Large amounts of manufactured goods were imported and Russia's own exports were largely agricultural produce (63 per cent) and timber (11 per cent). Moreover, Russia's industrial output was a long way behind that of the USA, Britain and Germany and on a per capita basis the gap was enormous. In fact, very few Russians worked in industry: Russia remained an overwhelmingly agrarian society – some 80 per cent worked on the land. The efficiency of Russian agriculture is a matter for debate but production certainly coped with the rapid population growth and there was a surplus for export.

'The great thrust towards modernization was state inspired and related to military needs' (Kennedy) and much of it was financed by heavy taxation. The social cost was considerable – while enormous sums went into rearmament very little went into health and education and there was little rise in living standards. Poor working and living conditions bred considerable discontent in a society in which politics did not really exist. Russia was ruled by a harsh autocracy which usually used force to suppress popular expression. The regime had little support even among the privileged, educated classes. However, discontent in the cities was not matched in the countryside and Russia in 1914 was a mixture of stability and instability. After the defeat in the war against Japan in 1905 and after the humiliation over Bosnia in 1908/9, rearmament became an urgent priority. But Russia's military forces remained more impressive on paper than in reality. Mobilisation and deployment were inefficient and whereas the Russian generals felt confident about the army's ability to confront Austria, they were less confident about their prospects against Germany.

Finally there was the ruler: Tsar Nicholas II was a less than impressive personality and the decision-making process in St Petersburg was bizarre, allowing anyone who could gain influence at court an opportunity to have a say in policy-making. All this would seem to suggest that Russia was not in reality a strong state, or at least not strong enough. Russia needed time to build up its strength, but time ran out in 1914.

Chronological survey of the period

1 The age of Bismarck 1871–90

The unification of Germany proclaimed in 1871 was in effect the conquest of the German states by Prussia. This had come about during the course of three wars in which Denmark (1864), Austria (1866) and France (1871) had all been defeated. Bismarck, the Chancellor of the new Germany, realised that his achievement had created a change in the balance of power in Germany's favour, which he sought to maintain. He did this by asserting that Germany was satisfied (i.e. it had no more ambitions), by keeping France isolated, and by being on good terms with both Austria and Russia.

He did this from 1879 by the method of creating a series of military alliances, a web of treaties that tied Austria, Russia and Italy to Germany (Great Britain would not be drawn). The major threat to peace in these years emanated from the Balkans where Turkish weakness was confronted with Balkan nationalism (this situation was often known as the 'Eastern Question'). Two crises involving Bulgaria (1877–8 and 1885–8) strained relations between Vienna and St Petersburg and Bismarck had to work hard to keep a foot in both camps.

Bismarck was an outstanding statesman and by the time he was forced to resign in 1890 he had successfully fulfilled his aims for a period of nearly 20 years (see profile on page 31).

2 Polarisation without tension 1890–1904

After Bismarck fell, the erratic Kaiser Wilhelm II gave German policy little coherence and the commanding position that Bismarck had achieved for Germany in international diplomacy was lost. Immediately, France and Russia came together and formed the military alliance (1892–4) that Bismarck had worked so hard to avoid. Now Germany was confronted with the possibility of war on two fronts and Count Alfred von Schlieffen drew up his famous plan to contend with this problem (see explanation on page 35 and Figure 5 on page 102). However, tension was not high in this era and there was little possibility of war.

One factor accounting for this was the good relations between Austria and Russia, particularly over the Eastern Question. Another crisis in this area in the mid 1890s failed to create any confrontation and in 1897 the Austrians and Russians agreed to maintain the status quo, while the latter turned their attention to the Far East. The Kaiser now embarked upon a policy of *Weltpolitik*, whereby Germany would acquire the trappings of a great power, an empire and a fleet. This venture could only upset Great Britain which was beginning to feel somewhat overstretched by all its commitments. However, Germany was not the enemy at this stage, France and Russia were, and many became convinced that a war between Britain and Russia was imminent.

3 A rise in tension 1904–13

War between Britain and Russia did not occur, but something of a diplomatic revolution did. First there was the Anglo–French *Entente* of 1904, then there was Russia's defeat by Japan in the war of 1904–5. This seriously undermined the balance of power in Germany's favour and the German government tried to take advantage of the situation by creating a crisis in Morocco in 1905 to humiliate France and break the *Entente*. However, German action had the opposite effect: the *Entente* was strengthened and Britain even made a deal with Russia in 1907.

German humiliation of Russia over the Bosnian crisis of 1909 also backfired when as a result Russia embarked upon a massive rearmament programme. Already Germany's naval building programme had created an armaments race with Britain, and a further crisis in Morocco in 1911 inspired the French to strengthen their army. The Germans and Austrians responded with Army Laws in 1912. Although the naval race came to an end, the continental powers were caught up in a spiral of ever-increasing rearmament, which the Germans came to believe would eventually give the *Entente* powers superiority. There was talk of a preventive war in Berlin.

Then the Eastern Question raised its ugly head again. Italy attacked Turkey in 1911 and its success inspired the Balkan states to fight two Balkan Wars – in 1912 and 1913 – the outcome of which was that Serbia doubled in size. This seriously unnerved the Austrians who came to see the ***panslavism*** of the Serbs as a direct threat to the integrity of their multi-ethnic empire. There was talk of a preventive war in Vienna too.

KEY TERM

Panslavism was the name given to the various movements for closer union of peoples speaking Slavic languages – a sense of ethnic solidarity.

4 The outbreak of war, 1914

This then was the background to the crisis that blew up in the summer of 1914. War was not inevitable and crises had been managed before; on this occasion, however, the crisis was used to make a conscious decision to wage war. The assassination of the heir to the Austrian throne in the Bosnian capital of Sarajevo on 28 June was Austria's opportunity to sort out the Serbs once and for all. Germany gave its full backing, prepared for either a diplomatic success or a continental war.

The crisis was slow to unfold and its seriousness did not become apparent until the end of July. Austria declared war on Serbia, and Russia, determined not to be humiliated as in 1909, mobilised its army as a gesture of support for the Serbs (but also confident of the support of the French). Russian mobilisation set off alarm bells in Berlin and in accordance with the Schlieffen Plan, Germany declared war on both Russia and France and invaded Belgium. The latter was used as an excuse by Britain to declare war on Germany, though its main concern remained the balance of power. The First World War had begun.

Kaiser WILHELM II, *1859–1941*

Grandson of Queen Victoria. Wilhelm II ruled Germany from 1888 until his abdication in 1918. He had had a difficult birth and was an erratic and unpredictable personality. After dismissing Bismarck he allowed policy to drift, though he favoured *Weltpolitik*, the establishment of a navy and the pursuit of empire. He advocated a tough line against Serbia in 1914 but once war broke out, power passed from him to the generals. After abdication he lived in Holland.

Helmuth von MOLTKE, *1848–1916*

Nephew of the great general whose victories enabled Prussia to unify Germany, Helmuth was appointed Chief of the General Staff in 1906 mainly because of his name. He held this position until his dismissal in September 1914. Although he was not really up to the job he was persuaded, despite ill health, to remain. If any one man can be held responsible for the First World War, it would be him. He advocated a preventive war from 1912 but only possessed a single plan of attack, the Schlieffen Plan, which he had modified in 1911 and in all probability weakened. Failure to achieve a quick victory in the West in 1914 led to a nervous breakdown and his dismissal. He died a broken man.

Theobald von BETHMANN HOLLWEG, *1856–1921*

German Chancellor from 1909 until his dismissal in 1917. Originally thought of as a moderating influence who was pushed by the generals, this view is no longer tenable. He took a 'calculated risk' in 1914 and was quite prepared for a full-scale war. Bethmann Hollweg was the author of the infamous 'September Programme' of German war aims which envisaged massive annexations and refused to consider peace negotiation once the Schlieffen Plan had failed.

Emperor Franz JOSEF I, *1830–1916*

Emperor of Austria from 1848 to 1916. He presided over the decline of his Empire as Austrian influence was removed from Italy and Germany (1859–66). His private life was tragic: his son committed suicide in 1889 and his wife was assassinated in 1898. The assassination of his heir and nephew, Archduke Franz Ferdinand, in Sarajevo in 1914 precipitated the First World War. He advocated an attack on Serbia. He was not quite the last Habsburg Emperor, that lot was to fall to his great nephew, Karl (Emperor 1916–18).

Franz, Count CONRAD von HÖTZENDORF, *1852–1925*

He became Chief of Staff of the Austro-Hungarian army in 1906. A vociferous advocate of aggressive war, this led to his dismissal in 1911, but he was reinstated in 1912. Hötzendorf advocated war against Serbia in 1914 but was not realistic about the capabilities of the army. He was dismissed by the Emperor Karl in 1916, by which time the Austrian army was subordinate to the German General Staff.

Tsar NICHOLAS II, *1868–1918*

The last Tsar of Russia (1894–1917) Nicholas II was a weak man with limited intelligence. He presided over defeat against the Japanese (1904–5), survived the so-called revolution of 1905, endured humiliation over the Bosnian Crisis of 1908–9 and by ordering mobilisation in July 1914 as a gesture of support for the Serbs, triggered Germany's declaration of war. He became Commander-in-Chief in 1915, but was forced to abdicate in 1917 as failure in the war had led to considerable unrest. He was executed by the Bolsheviks in 1918.

OTHER KEY FIGURES

Alois, Count Lexa von Aehrenthal, *1854–1912*
Austro-Hungarian Foreign Minister 1906–12; annexed Bosnia in 1908.

Prince Bernhard Heinrich von Bülow, *1849–1912*
German Foreign Secretary from 1897 and Chancellor 1900 to 1909.

Leopold, Count Berchtold, *1863–1942*
Austro-Hungarian Foreign Minister 1912–15; sent ultimatum to Serbia in 1914.

Erich von Falkenhayn, *1861–1922*
Prussian Minister of War 1913–15; Chief of the General Staff 1914–16.

Sir Edward Grey, *1862–1933*
British Foreign Secretary 1905–16; advocated intervention in 1914.

Paul von Hindenburg, *1847–1934*
Commander-in-Chief of the German army 1916–8 (later President of the Republic 1925–34).

Gottlieb von Jagow, *1863–1935*
German Foreign Secretary 1913–16.

Joseph Joffre, *1852–1931*
Commander-in-Chief of the French army from 1911 to 1916. Formulated Plan XVII and won the Battle of the Marne.

Erich von Ludendorff, *1865–1937*
Quartermaster General of the German army; number two to Hindenburg. He planned the 1918 offensive.

Raymond Poincaré, *1860–1934*
French Prime Minister 1912–13 and French President 1913–20.

Sergei Sazonov, *1861–1927*
Russia's Foreign Minister 1910–16. Cautious but advocated mobilisation in 1914.

PART TWO

CHAPTER ONE

HOW DID THE ALLIANCE SYSTEM COME ABOUT?

Objectives
◢ To look at the aims of Bismarck's foreign policy
◢ To decide how the alliance system came about
◢ To study the counter system and the Schlieffen Plan
◢ To explain the Diplomatic Revolution.

1871	German Empire proclaimed. France cedes Alsace-Lorraine
1878	Congress of Berlin
1879	Dual Alliance (Austria and Germany)
1881	Three Emperors' Alliance (Germany, Austria, Russia)
1882	Triple Alliance (Germany, Austria, Italy)
1887	Reinsurance Treaty (Germany, Russia)
1888	Wilhelm II becomes German Emperor
1890	Bismarck resigns
	Reinsurance Treaty lapses
1892–4	Franco–Russian Alliance
1897	Austro–Russian Agreement
1898	German Naval Law. Fashoda incident
1900	German Naval Law
1902	Anglo–Japanese Alliance
1903	Anti-Austrian coup in Serbia
1904	Russo–Japanese War (to 1905)
	Entente Cordiale (Britain and France)
1905	First Moroccan crisis
1906	Algeciras Conference
	Dreadnought launched
1907	Anglo-Russian *Entente*

The Bismarckian system, 1871–90

The aims of Bismarck's foreign policy
On 18 January 1871 in the Hall of Mirrors at the Palace of Versailles, the German Empire was proclaimed. Otto von Bismarck, the first

Chancellor of the new Germany, was sufficiently wise to realise that what had been so fortuitously created could just as easily be undone. Accordingly, his principal aim was to preserve what he had achieved, and the best way to do this was to maintain peace. After all, Germany had nothing to gain from another war; the new balance of power served it very well. Bismarck's objectives were to keep France isolated and to keep on good terms with both Austria and Russia. French defeat in 1870–71 had enabled the unification process to be completed, but Bismarck feared a revenge attack to recover Alsace-Lorraine (taken in the peace settlement of 1871). As far as Austria and Russia were concerned the German Chancellor favoured an *entente à trois:* he stated, 'all politics reduce themselves to this formula: try to be one of three, as long as the world is governed by an unstable equilibrium of five powers'.

Bismarck first tried to do this by means of a very loose arrangement, the **Three Emperors' League** (*Dreikaiserabkommen* 1873) by which the Emperors of Germany, Austria and Russia would meet informally to discuss matters of mutual interest. This was very much an Austro-Russian agreement which Germany joined later, but it served Bismarck's purpose well. It was not only a practical arrangement to keep republican France isolated, but also an ideological bond between conservative monarchs to resist radical politics (such as republicanism). However, the shortcomings of this somewhat fluid agreement were soon exposed in the **War-in-Sight** crisis of 1875. Bismarck, worried by France's rapid recovery, decided to intimidate it with a threat of war. The German press was encouraged to create a war scare (the headline of the *Berliner Post* posed the question, 'Is war in sight?') but the ruse backfired and the Tsar, Alexander II, took the side of the French. But if the Three Emperors' League foundered over this issue, it collapsed completely over the matter of the Eastern Question in 1878.

What was the Eastern Question?

The Eastern Question was about what should become of the declining Turkish Empire. Or, more specifically, what should be done in the Balkans about the decay of Turkish power in Europe. The Ottoman Empire, as it was also called (after its founder Osman), had been slowly contracting since the late seventeenth century. By the nineteenth century Turkey was known as the 'sick man of Europe', a phrase coined by Tsar Nicholas I, and its complete disintegration was believed to be imminent (incorrectly as it turned out). In the Balkans the Turks faced growing Balkan nationalism among the Slav peoples – Serbia and what became Rumania were autonomous by 1829 and the Greeks obtained actual independence in 1830 – and great power rivalry, particularly between Austria and Russia.

Austria (or more precisely Austria-Hungary as it was from 1867) was a multi-ethnic empire and therefore feared the growth of Slav nationalism as it could well undermine and threaten the monarchy's integrity. After all, Slavs made up about 46 per cent of the overall population (see Figure 1 on page 10). Given the Habsburg Empire's recent expulsion from both Italy and Germany, it did not wish to be expelled from the Balkans as well – here it would make a stand and expand.

Russia's principal concern, on the other hand, was the control of the Straits of the Bosphorus, which had immense strategic and economic importance (most of Russia's grain exports passed through here). It had long been an ambition of the Russian Tsars to win back Constantinople (Istanbul, the Turkish capital) for christianity. Russia was also a Slav state and had some sympathy for the people of the Balkans. Britain preferred to bolster Turkey and keep Russia out of the Mediterranean, whereas Bismarck had little interest in the area at all and, in a famous phrase, considered the Balkans 'not worth the healthy bones of a single Pomeranian musketeer'. However, he did realise that the Eastern Question was a threat to European stability and could not be ignored.

All in all, many felt the Balkans were a powderkeg waiting to explode, and it was not with much prescience that *Whitaker's Almanac* predicted each year that there would be 'trouble in the Balkans'.

The first Bulgarian crisis and the Congress of Berlin, 1878

A revolt in Bosnia in 1875 was followed by a revolt in Bulgaria in 1876, political upheaval in Constantinople and declarations of war by Serbia and Montenegro. Turkish success in crushing the opposition presented

Austria and Russia with a formidable problem but one which they appeared to have solved – until the beginning of 1878. Basically, Russia went to war with Turkey in 1877 with Austrian approval on the understanding that no large Slav state would be created. However, in 1878, flushed with success, the Russians went back on their agreement and by the Treaty of San Stefano created a large Bulgaria. Clearly San Stefano was 'a treaty too far' (Bartlett). Austria (and Britain) were outraged and the powers decided to settle the matter at a congress, chaired reluctantly by Bismarck, in Berlin.

By the Treaty of Berlin the big Bulgaria was dismantled; Macedonia was returned to Turkey and the remaining area was divided into a small autonomous Bulgaria and an autonomous Eastern Rumelia (see Figure 2 on page 26). In addition, Serbia and Rumania gained independence, Britain obtained Cyprus and Austria obtained a **protectorate** over Bosnia. Although Russia recovered Bessarabia, the treaty was clearly a defeat for it. Checking Russian pretensions obviously made sense in European terms, but the settlement was not realistic for the Balkans and it did not last long.

KEY TERM

Protectorate – a country that is under the official protection and partial control of a stronger one.

Bismarck, who had tried to stay out of the whole affair, was now blamed by the Russians for their diplomatic defeat. Moreover, Russo–German relations worsened over economic matters as each power sought to protect its interests by putting up **tariff barriers**. What was Bismarck to do? 'The crisis of 1878–9 had shown that the loose diplomatic arrangements characteristic of the 1870s could not give Germany adequate security' (Bridge and Bullen). The years 1879 to 1882 were to mark a decisive change.

KEY TERM

Tariff barriers are taxes on imports to protect native produce.

Figure 2 The growth of Balkan independence, 1822–1913 (dates refer to the year in which independence was gained from Turkey)

The birth of the alliance system

What Bismarck's exact motives were in forging an alliance with Austria in 1879 remain elusive, but it is clear that he felt German security to be threatened and that a military alliance with Austria would at least tie one of the powers to him. But the truth is he acted on the spur of the moment and saw the alliance as only a temporary expedient. His real objective remained a revival of the Three Emperors' League. Yet the **Dual Alliance** of 1879 became a keystone of German foreign policy and was renewed regularly down to 1918.

It was 'the first of the secret treaties whose contents were never fully known but always suspected' (Gordon Craig, *Germany 1866-1945*, Oxford, 1978) and it proved to be the genesis of a new system of formal alliances.

The Dual Alliance, October 1879 (and renewed regularly thereafter)

Germany and Austria-Hungary promised mutual aid if either of them were attacked by Russia and benevolent neutrality in case of an attack by another power. This treaty was aimed at Russia but it was essentially defensive. It was to last five years.

Although the Dual Alliance was essentially a defensive arrangement, it was aimed at Russia and this fact was leaked to the Russians, to bring home their isolation. The ploy worked; the Russian government was soon anxious for an understanding and with the retirement in 1880 of Prince Alexander Gorchakov, the Russian Foreign Minister (and a personal enemy of the German Chancellor), the way was open for a reconciliation.

In June 1881, the **Three Emperors' Alliance** (the *Dreikaiserbund*) was signed. 'I knew that the Russians would come to us once we had pinned the Austrians down' said Bismarck and his gamble proved correct.

The Three Emperors' Alliance, June 1881 renewed 1884

Austria, Germany and Russia guaranteed to be neutral if any of the three should find themselves at war with a fourth Great Power. This was clearly aimed at France. The treaty also included a vague understanding about the annexation of Bosnia by Austria and the union of Bulgaria and Eastern Rumelia, both at an unspecified date in the future. This embodied Bismarck's idea of spheres of influence in the Balkans (i.e. Austria in the West, Russia in the East).

Then in 1882 quite by chance Bismarck gained another ally, Italy. Outraged by the French occupation of Tunis in 1881, the Italians approached Bismarck and after reaching agreement with Vienna, the Triple Alliance was signed in May 1882. Thus in the short space of three years Bismarck had so enhanced Germany's position that Berlin was now regarded as the diplomatic capital of Europe and his secret alliances gave him a measure of control over all European politics.

The Triple Alliance, May 1882, renewed February 1887

This was formed between Austria, Italy and Germany and was to last five years. It was essentially defensive. Italy and Germany were to help each other if either was attacked by France. Austria would also help Italy against France, but Italy would only help Austria against Russia if France joined the latter. Clearly this treaty was aimed at France.

Other alliances were signed with Serbia in 1881 and Rumania in 1883 but the *Dreikaiserbund* remained the most important treaty, around which the 'European states system continued to revolve' (Bridge and Bullen). When it was renewed in 1884 it proved to be the zenith of the Bismarckian system.

With Europe supposedly under control, Bismarck now branched out into the colonial sphere, acquiring South West Africa, Togoland, the Cameroons, German East Africa and some Pacific islands in 1884 and

1885. He did not set much store by colonies but saw colonial rivalry as a good way to divert European rivalry, and a way of improving relations with France. However, all this was short-lived as another Bulgarian crisis erupted.

The second Bulgarian crisis, 1885–8

The second Bulgarian crisis is very complicated and it would be better not to get too bogged down in detail. The important points to remember are that although it destroyed the Three Emperors' Alliance, Bismarck was able to salvage an understanding with the Russians by signing the Reinsurance Treaty in 1887, and keep the peace by restraining both Austria and Russia. By the mid 1880s the Great Powers' position of 1878 had been completely reversed. Because the Bulgarians had shown themselves to be anything but Russian puppets, Austria and Britain now favoured a big Bulgaria, whereas, for the same reason, Russia did not. In September 1885, Prince Alexander of Bulgaria declared the union of Bulgaria with Eastern Rumelia. He did this without consulting the Russians, who were furious. However, the *Dreikaiserbund* held together and in 1886 the reality of a big Bulgaria was accepted (despite the complication of a short war between Serbia and Bulgaria). However, in August and September 1886 a Russian conspiracy eventually led to Alexander's abdication. Austria was now furious and Austro–Russian relations deteriorated rapidly. Indeed by November open threats of war were made in Vienna. At the same time (to complicate the issue further) in France, the rise of General Boulanger, who favoured a war of revenge against Germany, unnerved Bismarck who was also concerned about the possibility of a Franco–Russian rapprochement. A general war now seemed a real possibility.

In February 1887 Bismarck worked hard to renew the Triple Alliance but had to concede terms more favourable to Italy; at the same time the First Mediterranean Agreement was signed between Britain, Italy and Austria to maintain the status quo in the Mediterranean. Both developments kept France in check and the general situation improved when the French dropped Boulanger from the cabinet and adopted a more cautious policy. However, by the spring of 1887 it was apparent that the Russians would not renew the Three Emperors' League, and Bismarck again had to work hard to keep a foot in both camps. Thus in June 1887 he signed a bipartite agreement with Russia – the

Reinsurance Treaty – that kept discussions going with St Petersburg as well as Vienna. This treaty has been described as Bismarck's master-piece, but he only saw it as a temporary measure to shore up a difficult situation.

> **The Reinsurance Treaty, June 1887**
>
> This was signed between Russia and Germany and stated that each would remain neutral if the other went to war with a third power, but the agreement would not become operative if Germany attacked France or if Russia attacked Austria-Hungary.

However, the situation in the Balkans did not improve. In July 1887 the Bulgars elected Ferdinand of Saxe-Coburg as prince – against the wishes of the Russians. Bismarck broke off diplomatic relations with Bulgaria to please Russia, while at the same time he restrained Russia by cutting off any further loans in November and by encouraging the Second Mediterranean Agreement in December. In this, Britain, Austria and Italy agreed to maintain the status quo in the Near East.

Bismarck worked hard to keep the peace and in February 1888 he published the Dual Alliance to make it clear that this was a defensive alliance, to restrain both Austria and Russia. Finally, in March 1888, the situation was defused when the Russians contented themselves with a Turkish declaration that Ferdinand's election was illegal, though Ferdinand remained in place. Peace had been preserved.

This was to be Bismarck's last foreign policy success. 'When William II ascended the throne in July 1888 the sands began to run out quickly for Bismarck' (William Carr, *A History of Germany 1815–1990*, Arnold, 1987) – the new Kaiser was determined to rule as well as reign and he had very different ideas about foreign policy. It was also clear that France and Russia were moving closer together; however, in June 1890 when the Reinsurance Treaty was up for renewal, Tsar Alexander III was keen for it to be renewed. But BISMARCK had resigned in March, forced out by the new Emperor.

◢ Source

Bulgaria, that little country between the Danube and the Balkans, is not by any means a matter of sufficient importance to justify an all-European war from Moscow to the Pyrenees and from the North Sea to Palermo; at the end of such a war nobody would know just what he had fought for.

Bismarck to the Reichstag, February 1888

Profile
PRINCE OTTO VON BISMARCK   1815–1898

Bismarck was born in 1815 at Schönhausen in Prussia and studied law and agriculture as a student. In the 1850s he was Prussia's representative at the German diet in Frankfurt where he came to resent Austrian dominance. After being ambassador to Russia (1859–62) and briefly to Paris, he was recalled in 1862 to become Minister President to solve a funding crisis. He solved it by collecting taxes and building up the army without recourse to the Chamber. Bismarck aimed to extend Prussia both in terms of influence and territory and in three wars – against Denmark (1864), Austria (1866) and France (1870–71) – he took the opportunity to unify Germany. As Chancellor of the new Germany from 1871 to 1890 he dominated international affairs and while he was less successful in domestic matters (his campaigns against Catholics and Socialists were failures), when he died in 1898, the Times *of London concluded that he was the man of the century (with Napoleon a close second).*

Analysis: was there a Bismarckian system?

It would appear that the alliance system was the brainchild of just one man, Otto von Bismarck. But it is important not to make Bismarck appear cleverer than he actually was. Much was decided in other European capitals and other powers did not simply dance to the German Chancellor's tune: they pursued their own interests (e.g. Italy in the renewal of the Triple Alliance in 1887) and often forced Bismarck to be involved in matters which he did not wish to be involved in (e.g. the Balkans). Moreover, alliances were not the sum total of Bismarck's foreign policy. He was constantly involved in a wide variety of diplomatic activities – indeed his policies often took so many twists and turns that they are frequently difficult to follow. He was, to use his own phrase, a man 'with many irons in the fire'.

Many of his moves were ad hoc, that is to say temporary, reactive, designed to meet an immediate problem. He saw the Dual Alliance as a temporary expedient (but it became permanent); the Triple Alliance was not of his own making and the *Dreikaiserbund*, the keystone of his policy, only lasted about five years.

Yet, if even only inadvertently, Bismarck did create a system where one power tied several others to it and thereby enjoyed a preponderance. He was able to keep the peace; he did fulfil his aims.

Whether the alliances were actually necessary is questionable. Bismarck seems to have been driven by immense insecurity. So much so that towards the end of his period of office his 'system' was becoming increasingly complex and even contradictory. Indeed Friedrich von Holstein, an official at the German Foreign Office, described the Reinsurance Treaty as 'political bigamy', and it does seem that Bismarck was playing a double game, trying to be friends with two enemies, Austria and Russia, while making out he was only on the side of one.

Was he successful?

There is no doubt that Bismarck fulfilled his basic aims. He kept the peace, kept France isolated and kept a dialogue going with both Vienna and St Petersburg. However, it must be acknowledged that French isolation had a lot to do with its own internal political weakness; and that the maintenance of peace in general had much to do with the fact that the other Great Powers did not want to risk a major war either. Nevertheless, it is true to say that there was much discussion of war in late 1887 and many even within the German military and Foreign Office were advocating war with Russia. Bismarck restrained them. It is quite clear that the Eastern Question represented the greatest threat to European peace and it is also clear that in both 1878 and 1886 it was Russia which caused the greatest upset.

How do recent historians rate Bismarck's foreign policy? The British historian, W. N. Medlicott, was not impressed – he felt that Bismarck's balance of tensions 'had made a deadlock and called it peace'. In short, he created greater tensions. Otto Pflanze, the German biographer, on the other hand, feels that Bismarck's system controlled tensions in a volatile and unpredictable situation.

And what of the end of his period of office? Was the so-called 'Second Bismarckian System' of 1887 a contradiction or crowning achievement? William Carr described Bismarck's policy as being 'virtually in ruin' – an assessment echoed by Bridge and Bullen who simply state: 'Bismarck had failed; and he left his successors a *damnosa hereditas*'. Gordon Craig, on the other hand, is more positive: Bismarck 'could take satisfaction in the fact that his network of alliances was still in good repair ... there was no immediate prospect of new troubles in Europe'. It seems that far too much criticism of Bismarck is based on hindsight. Thus he is blamed for the subsequent polarisation of Europe and even for the First World War. However, he cannot be blamed for the mistakes of his successors, although it is true to say that the creation of a formal military alliance system could (and did) lead to a counter-system. But whether this made war more or less likely is a moot point.

A counter-system: fluidity to polarisation, 1890–1907

The Franco–Russian Alliance, 1894

We now move into a more fluid states system that is difficult to categorise. To begin with it is important to say something about the personality of Kaiser Wilhelm II, because he was to have a profound effect on subsequent events. He had been deprived of oxygen during delivery and had been born with a withered arm. It seems that because of the former he was unstable. Sir Edward Grey described him as 'a battleship ... with no rudder' and Waldersee, the German Commander-in-Chief (until 1891), stated that he was 'extraordinarily restless ... gives countless and often contradictory orders, and scarcely listens to advisers'. All who met him agreed that something was not quite right about the Kaiser. He had a firm belief in divine-right monarchy and saw himself as the warrior prince; however, he was incapable of the hard work necessary to formulate policy and the military wielded an inordinate influence over him. The historian John Röhl has characterised him as a 'manic depressive' which meant that he could either be immovable on a subject during a period of mania, or easily persuaded when in a state of depression.

What all this meant was that German foreign policy came to be characterised by a restless ambition and by a degree of incoherence and unpredictability. Whereas Bismarck had stated as late as 1890 that 'we have no demands to make', this was not going to be the position under the Kaiser. There was to be a 'new course'.

One of the Kaiser's first moves was to allow the Reinsurance Treaty to lapse, in June 1890. This, together with his (unsuccessful) approaches to Britain, pushed the Russians into the arms of the French, thereby creating a counter-alliance and achieving exactly what Bismarck had always sought to avoid. Of course Russia and France had already been growing closer together. Bismarck had stopped loans to Russia forcing it to borrow in Paris (October 1888) and in January 1889 the Russians had bought French rifles. In August 1891, an *entente* was negotiated, followed by a military convention in 1892 and a full-blown **alliance** in 1894. There was, however, nothing inevitable about this alliance – a conservative autocracy and a republic were strange bedfellows – and it should be remembered that the Tsar was eager to renew the Reinsurance Treaty in 1890; it was the change in German policy that allowed the alliance to take place. Now Germany was faced with the possibility of war on two fronts and accordingly Count Alfred von Schlieffen (Commander-in-Chief 1891–1905) began work on his famous plan which was to play such a crucial role in turning a Balkan crisis into a major war in 1914.

Franco–Russian Alliance, 1894, renewed 1899

If France were attacked by Germany, or by Italy supported by Germany, Russia would attack Germany; alternatively, if Russia were attacked by Germany or by Austria-Hungary supported by Germany, France would attack Germany. If any member of the Triple Alliance mobilised, then France and Russia would automatically mobilise.

The renewal provided for mutual support against Britain: France would move 100,000 soldiers to the Channel coast, Russia the same number to the frontiers of India.

The Schlieffen Plan

Count Alfred von Schlieffen was Chief of the German General Staff from 1891 to 1905. In attempting to solve the problem of a two-front war he proposed a rapid, decisive opening blow against France, by a flanking movement through Holland and Belgium, which would achieve success in just six weeks (success had been achieved in six weeks in 1870). Having defeated France, the army would then transfer to the Eastern Front to fight the Russians who, lacking a sufficient railway network, would take at least six weeks to mobilise fully. The plan emerged in the 1890s and was finalised in 1905–6. However, by 1911 Moltke the younger, Schlieffen's successor, had so modified the plan – by weakening the right wing, abandoning the sweep through Holland, and strengthening the left – that the whole *raison d'être* of Schlieffen's Plan (drawing the French army into Lorraine, having sufficient soldiers on the right to surround Paris) was completely lost (see Figure 5 on page 102).

The Eastern Question again

The new Franco–Russian alliance did not, in fact, lead to the formation of two hostile camps as both Germany and Austria sought to remain on good terms with Russia and European interests were channelled into imperial questions in Africa and Asia. Indeed the country that seemed to have most to fear from the Franco–Russian alliance was Great Britain because of mutual imperial rivalries (see below). One aspect of the reasonable calm pervading international relations at this time was the peaceful resolution of yet another Eastern Question crisis (1894–7).

A rising of Armenian christians provoked Turkish massacres. Britain was concerned to intervene but the Russians were reluctant (they had a sizeable Armenian minority of their own). When unrest continued and spread, the powers began to talk about the possibility of Turkish disintegration and a partition. However, all talk of this was premature, as the Turks demonstrated by a rapid defeat of Greece in the spring of 1897. In the face of Franco–Russian solidarity there was little Britain could do and Lord Salisbury, the Prime Minister, decided that the preservation of Turkey was beyond the Royal Navy's capability. It would not be possible to protect Turkey from Russia and fight France at the same time. So Salisbury decided to abandon the Mediterranean Agreement with Austria and concentrate on control of Egypt as a better way of looking after Britain's interest in the Near East. As France was also in favour of maintaining the status quo, Russia decided restraint was the best policy. With the abandonment of the Mediterranean Agreement, Austria now turned to Russia and made a deal in May 1897 whereby they would both uphold the status quo in the Near East. What this last agreement demonstrated was the fluidity and flexibility of Great Power relations at this time. It was quite possible for Austria and Russia to sign an agreement despite being in contrary alliance systems. It made sense for the two powers with the greatest interest in the Eastern Question to reach agreement on the matter.

Weltpolitik

The agreement between Austria and Russia was one of a number of bilateral agreements signed over the next few years that cut across the respective alliances – such as the Franco–Italian agreements of 1899, 1900 and 1902 (these in effect nullified the Triple Alliance and proved to be permanent), the Austro–Italian agreement of 1899 and a further Austro–Russian agreement in 1903. Indeed in 1904 when Russia went to war with Japan, Austria declared neutrality. All of these arrangements suggested that the Dual and Triple Alliances had virtually ceased to exist. Germany, meanwhile, had embarked upon a policy of Weltpolitik (which means 'world policy').

Germany was a world power without the trappings of a world power and the Kaiser felt Germany should have an empire and a fleet appropriate to its economic and military status. Already in 1896 with the Krüger telegram, Wilhelm II had intervened in South Africa in a move designed to insult Britain. 'Radical nationalists shared William's resentment of Britain and welcomed the ostentatious gesture of protest as a sign that Germany was now playing her rightful role in world politics' (Carr). Then in 1897 the Germans took over the Chinese port of Kiao-Chow (the other powers responded); in 1898 several Spanish Pacific islands were purchased and the Kaiser toured the Ottoman Empire indicating he was their true friend (and later was the driving force behind a Berlin–Baghdad railway). In 1899 part of the Samoan islands were taken over and in 1898 and 1900 two navy bills were passed, the first proposing 19 battleships, the second doubling that number. Clearly the development of a fleet was aimed against Britain, but at the turn of the century Britain was more concerned about France and Russia.

Imperial rivalry

In 1898 at Fashoda in the Sudan, Britain and France had clashed and the French had had to back down. There was much talk of war. The French military drew up invasion plans of Britain, and when the Franco–Russian alliance was renewed in 1899 it was specifically aimed at Britain. Britain was also concerned about Russian expansion in the Far East: in 1898 the Russians had leased Port Arthur and in 1900 they invaded the province of Manchuria. All this made Britain inclined to look to Germany for an agreement and between 1898 and 1901 three approaches were made. However, Germany had no interest in making a deal over Britain's interests in the Far East, just as Britain was not prepared to commit itself to Germany's interests in Europe. German thinking was based on the false assumption that Great Britain's difficulties with France and Russia would grow. In fact, the Germans became convinced that a war between Russia and Great Britain was imminent. The scene was set for a diplomatic revolution.

The Diplomatic Revolution (1902–7) and the first Moroccan crisis (1905–6)

When Britain made an alliance with Japan in 1902 aimed at Russia, the Germans were convinced that this made war in the Far East more likely. France too thought along the same lines and now became anxious about the possibility of being dragged into this war as an ally of Russia. At the same time Morocco fell into anarchy and civil war and Paul Delcassé, the French Foreign Minister, was keen to establish French control. Accordingly, he saw the possibility of negotiating an understanding with Britain as the best solution to these problems. Britain was ready to listen and although the process was slow, negotiations got under way after Edward VII's state visit in 1903. The outbreak of the Russo–Japanese war in February 1904, led to the signing of the *Entente Cordiale* in April 1904. It was not a military alliance, just a resolution of colonial differences, not unlike many of the other bilateral agreements recently signed. France recognised Britain in Egypt and Britain would support French claims to Morocco. Germany was not unduly concerned about this agreement and believed it would not last. The *Entente* was an important psychological reconciliation but it was only subsequent events that turned it into something more.

The Anglo–Japanese Alliance, 1902

If either were involved in a war with a third power, the other would observe strict neutrality; if either were involved in war with two powers, then the other would lend assistance. This was regularly renewed down to 1922.

The most significant event to influence international relations at this time was the **Russo–Japanese War of 1904–5**. The defeat of Russia was a decisive event which changed the balance of power quite dramatically. During the course of the war Germany had offered Russia a defensive alliance against Britain, but Britain and Russia had no wish to fight each other and German calculations had gone awry. However, from the German point of view the outcome of the war was quite favourable. Russia was a broken reed, the possibility of a two-front war had evaporated and France was also weakened. Up to 1905 German policy had been characterised by drift as it awaited events to occur in its favour – but this had not really happened. Now, in 1905, Germany adopted a more aggressive stance and decided to put pressure on France, in Morocco.

In March 1905, Kaiser Wilhelm II landed in Tangier and declared Morocco independent. The French were forced to agree to an international conference on the matter and the French cabinet decided to sacrifice Delcassé to defuse the situation. So menacing was Germany's tone that for the first time the British defence departments began to look seriously at the implications of war with Germany. In July the Kaiser signed a draft agreement with the Tsar at Björkö. Suddenly, Germany's apparently strong position fell apart. The Björkö agreement was not ratified by either government (the Russians were loyal to France and did not want to be Germany's junior partner), Britain and France began a series of informal military discussions and at the Algeciras Conference in January 1906 called to discuss Morocco, the

Germans found themselves confronted by Britain, France and Russia. So far from breaking the *Entente*, German intervention in Morocco had only succeeded in strengthening it. Now the Russians agreed to the French proposal to drop the Dual Alliance clauses against Britain. This opened the way for a reconciliation between Britain and Russia.

Now that Japan had defeated Russia, Britain no longer feared it and was quite prepared to reach an agreement (31 August 1907) which took the form of a settlement of a number of disputes. In particular, Russia renounced its interests in Afghanistan, and Persia was divided into spheres of influence. But for Sir Edward Grey, the British Foreign Minister, the agreement was a weapon against the domination of Europe by Germany. These diplomatic setbacks for Germany engendered immense frustration in Berlin. Talk of the inevitability of war began to resurface; Germany was surrounded by hostile powers and was no longer able to exploit the rivalries of others. There was quite a discrepancy between Germany's strong economic and military power and its weak diplomatic position. Meanwhile, Britain had been able to come to terms with its erstwhile enemies, France and Russia. This was a remarkable turnabout but of course the agreements were not military and they need not have been permanent. It would be wrong to see Europe as divided into two hostile camps, even at this late stage.

Analysis: post-Bismarck, 1890–1907

With the establishment of a rival counter-alliance between France and Russia in 1894 the potential for polarisation and confrontation was created, but did not occur. What is remarkable about these years is the fluidity and flexibility of international relations. That a number of bilateral agreements could be made that cut across the existing alliances is testimony to that fact. Moreover, rivalries tended to be played out outside Europe, in Africa and the Far East, where confrontation could be avoided and compromise could be reached. In addition, the primary European problem, the Eastern Question, was to some extent put on ice by the Austro–Russian *Entente*. It would be too simplistic to state that Russia turned away completely from the Balkans to concentrate on the Far East but there is an element of truth in this.

The one country that felt increasingly insecure in these years was Great Britain. Its worldwide commitments and its isolation, together with specific problems with France and Russia, led it to seek an understanding with both these powers and to abandon its traditional defence of Turkey. The wild card in the pack remained Germany. Under the Kaiser, unpredictability, bouts of activity and inactivity seemed to mirror Wilhelm's personality – the new course, the free hand, *Weltpolitik* ... Germany did not find its place in the sun and its position relative to the other powers seemed to deteriorate. Germany's involvement in the Far East and in the Ottoman Empire created concern in both St Petersburg and Vienna, and its decision to build a navy had, by 1903, begun to cause some concern in London. Moreover, the expectation that Britain would remain in opposition to France and Russia, and even go to war with the latter, was completely confounded by events. However, until 1905 German policy was not aggressive and *Weltpolitik* and the new navy were not the prime causes of Britain's reconciliation with France and Russia (though Germany's indifference to Britain had given Parliament little alternative). Unlike in Bismarck's time, Germany did not take the leading role in international relations. When it tried to do so, it picked the wrong moment.

At the end of our period the collapse of Russian power created an imbalance of power which Germany tried to take advantage of, without success. Britain stepped in to fill the gap. The outcome was a frustrated Germany, and in London and Paris at least, some concern and suspicion about Germany's future plans. German aggression had introduced an element of instability into the volatile mix of international relations. If it continued, polarisation would only increase.

Summary
So, how did the alliance system come about? Indeed, was there an alliance system as such by the end of our period? The alliance system was created, albeit inadvertently, by Bismarck to protect the new Germany. He tried to remain on good terms with both Vienna and St Petersburg and keep France isolated. Once he left office a rival alliance, the Franco–Russian Alliance, was allowed to occur, but this did not lead to polarisation and confrontation. Outside the system, Britain escaped complete isolation by making agreements (but not alliances) with France and Russia, but still there was no major crisis until Russia's defeat by the Japanese in 1905. This to some extent destroyed the balance of power in Europe and Germany's aggressive attempt to take

advantage of this situation in Morocco did lead to a degree of polarisation at the end of our period. But we do not as yet have two armed camps, ready to go to war – even if the potential was there.

WARNING!

The first half of this chapter will be useful if you are answering questions on Bismarck's foreign policy. However, when answering questions on the outbreak of the First World War, you should be careful not to get too bogged down in a discussion of the alliance systems, particularly with regard to the 1870s and 1880s (unless the question specifically requires you to do so). Remember your time is limited. Too many candidates never reach 1900, let alone 1914. This detailed chapter is essentially one of background, though the polarisation that occurs after Bismarck does have important long-term significance.

Documentary sources

The format

Documentary sources at A-level tend to be contemporary sources and the object of the exercise is, usually, to test **recall, comprehension, comparison and evaluation.**

An initial question might simply use the source as a prompt to test **recall** (i.e. memory/knowledge) by, for instance, referring to a historical figure in the source and asking his position in government.

A second question might ask you to explain a source (i.e. **comprehension**) by expressing its content in a succinct and simplified way, or it might require you to **evaluate** its usefulness. This would require you to analyse the content and possibly determine whether or not it is reliable – though even unreliable sources can be useful if you are aware of their unreliability (e.g. propaganda may give a false message but at least it tells you what false message someone is trying to get across).

However, do not fall into the trap of giving a stock answer (i.e. 'but this document might be biased ...') when you do not really know whether or not it is. You might be missing the point; many documents used in these exercises are reliable and you can take them at face value. The art of doing well is knowing what you can and cannot trust.

Yet another question might require you to **compare** two or three sources to determine which is/are more useful, or how it might be possible to reconcile or explain seemingly contradictory statements. Again an evaluation of the content is necessary and an assessment of reliability is sometimes (but not always) necessary – as indeed is your knowledge of the topic. Sometimes it is appropriate to inject your own knowledge or refer to another document.

A final question usually asks a general question which you have to answer by referring to all the sources (and you should always do this by referring to all the sources *by letter or number throughout*) and by employing your own knowledge. Documentary exercises vary considerably both in terms of the number and types of sources and in the question asked, but recall, comprehension, comparison and evaluation will probably be common to them all.

Exercise

EUROPEAN DIPLOMACY, 1905–1907

Study Documents I, II and III below and then answer questions **1** to **6** which follow:

Document I

On August 12th [1905], the British and Japanese Governments renewed their agreements of January 30th, 1902 ... Henceforth England can count on the armies of the Mikado[1] for the defence of her Indian Empire and the adjoining countries, namely, Tibet, Afghanistan and Persia. When informing us of this treaty ... the British Secretary of State asked us 'as a great favour' to help him in preventing the Russians from putting an undesirable construction upon it ... He wrote ... 'Our compact with Japan in no way excludes the idea of a friendly understanding with Russia covering the future development of our policy in those regions where the interests of the two powers are in contact.'

In my talk with Rouvier[2] I supported the British request ... reminding him of ... all we know of William II's subterranean intrigues against us at the Tsar's court. [I said] 'It is a matter of great concern ... to us that Russia shall gradually get on to a footing of collaboration with England. Otherwise, the bonds of Russo–German friendship will draw closer and closer – which will mean the end of the Franco–Russian alliance.'

Maurice Paléologue, senior French diplomat, in his memoirs, published in 1934.

Document II

The Entente with France means good and easy relations for both of us with Italy and Spain ... To complete this foundation, we wish to make an arrangement with Russia that will remove the old traditions of enmity, and ensure that, if we are not close friends, at any rate we do not quarrel. If all this can be done, we shall take care that it is not used to provoke Germany, or to score off her, if she will only accept it, and not try to make

---

[1]The Mikado was the Emperor of Japan.
[2]Rouvier was the French Prime Minister.

mischief ... The economic rivalry ... with Germany does not give much offence to our people, and they admire her steady industry and genius for organisation. But they do resent mischief-making ... They suspect the Emperor of aggressive plans of <u>Weltpolitik</u>, and they see or think they see that Germany is forcing the pace in armaments in order to dominate Europe, and is thereby laying a horrible burden of wasteful expenditure upon all the other Powers.

Sir Edward Grey, Foreign Secretary, in a confidential letter to President Theodore Roosevelt, December 1906.

Document III

In August 1907, a treaty on the partition of spheres of influence in Asia had been arranged between Russia and England ... <u>Fundamentally the treaty was more favourable to the Russians than to the English</u> ... That such an arrangement could be concluded proved ... that we had now become the chief object of English anxieties and jealousy: that England was ready to make considerable sacrifices in order to be secure against us.

Prince von Bülow, reporting the views he had expressed to the Kaiser, in his Memoirs, 1930.

1 In the context of these Documents, explain briefly what you understand by:
   a) 'The Entente with France'
   b) 'Weltpolitik'. (2)

2 Why, according to the author of Document I, was it important to France 'that Russia shall gradually get on to a footing of collaboration with England'? (2)

3 How do Documents I and III differ in the reasons they state, or imply, for British attempts to come to an agreement with Russia? (3)

4 To what extent does a consideration of the tone and contents of Documents II and III suggest that later German claims about 'encirclement' were justified? (5)

5 Noting their origins, which of Documents I and II do you consider gives the more reliable account of its country's foreign policy interests and concerns in 1905–1906? Explain your answer by reference to both Documents. (6)

6 Using these Documents, and your own knowledge, how far do you agree with Prince von Bülow's assessment of the terms of the Anglo–Russian Treaty of 1907 given in Document III: 'Fundamentally the treaty was more favourable to the Russians than to the English'? **(7)**

ULEAC 1995

CHAPTER TWO

WHY DID THE PRINCIPAL SOURCES OF TENSION BETWEEN 1905 AND 1913 NOT LEAD TO WAR?

Objectives

◢ To study the principal sources of tension in the years preceding the First World War

◢ To examine the Balkans Wars, 1912–13, and to ascertain if they contributed to instability in Europe

◢ To examine why a major war did not break out before 1914.

1905	First Moroccan crisis
1906	Algeciras Conference
	'Dreadnought' launched
1907	Anglo–Russian *Entente*
1908	German Naval Law
	Austria annexes Bosnia
1909	German ultimatum to Russia ends Bosnian crisis
1911	Second Moroccan crisis
	Italo–Turkish War (to 1912)
1912	First Balkan War
1913	Second Balkan War

The principal sources of tension in these years were the two Moroccan crises of 1905 and 1911, the Anglo–German naval rivalry (circa 1906–12) and the return of the Eastern Question in 1908–9 and 1911–13.

The first Moroccan crisis of 1905

This event was dealt with in Chapter 1 but the question arises, why did it not lead to hostilities? After all, with Russia defeated by Japan and paralysed by revolution, there could not have been a better time for Germany to deal with France. The situation was much more favourable than 1914 when Russia had recovered and Britain had committed itself in principle to a continental strategy. The German army was ready for war. Schlieffen, the Chief of Staff, who was working on the December memorandum which was to be the most complete formulation of his plan, was in a warlike mood – and it is likely he had the full support of Holstein at the Foreign Office. These men had little time for *Weltpolitik* – the policy of the Chancellor (Count Bernard von Bülow) and the Minister for Marine (Admiral Alfred von Tirpitz) – believing that continental domination came before world policy. In December Holstein, when speaking of the forthcoming Algeciras Conference, stated that the outcome would be either 'a heavy loss of prestige ... or an armed conflict'. But the truth is neither the Kaiser nor his Chancellor thought along these lines at the time. They hoped to break the *Entente* and achieve a diplomatic victory – and the result was humiliation at Algeciras. The French got exactly what they wanted: the *Entente* was strengthened and the Germans were isolated except for the support of Austria. This, to some extent, explains why Germany was so supportive of Austria when the next Balkan crisis occurred.

Of course it is also true to say that the other powers did not want war. In fact this crisis came out of the blue and so unnerved Paris and London that the French dropped Delcassé and agreed to a conference, while the British for the first time began seriously to consider how they might fight a continental war at short notice. In 1907 the British government committed itself to the creation of a small expeditionary force.

The Bosnian crisis 1908–9

Despite the Austro–Russian agreements of 1897 and 1903, time had not stood still in the Balkans. There had been growing German economic penetration of the Ottoman Empire of which the Berlin–Baghdad railway (subject to agreements of 1899 and 1903) was probably the most prominent manifestation, and there had been considerable unrest in Macedonia. Turkey still held a considerable amount of territory in Europe – Albania, Thrace and Macedonia which consisted of the three provinces of Kossovo, Monastir and Salonika. However, the major powers were disinclined to do much about the people there other than propose some mild reform of Turkish government which the Sultan was able to ignore. However, fear that Macedonia would be lost did lead to the **Young Turk Revolution** of July 1908 which weakened Turkey at a crucial moment.

KEY TERM

The **Young Turk Revolution** was a liberal reform movement among young army officers in the Ottoman Empire. The rebellion of 1908 led to constitutional rule.

What proved to be the most dangerous development in these years was the change in government in Belgrade. In June 1903, the pro-Austrian King Alexander of Serbia was murdered and replaced by the Russophile King Peter who was determined to reduce Austrian influence. This raised considerable fears in Vienna where it was felt a really independent Serbia might become the nucleus of a large south Slav state which might threaten the very existence of the multi-ethnic Habsburg Empire. A tariff war began in 1905–6, and the Serbs turned to France for arms and finance. In 1906 the uncompromising and aggressive Baron Aehrenthal became Austrian Foreign Minister and he was determined to weaken or even destroy Serbia. At the beginning of 1908 he proposed a railway in the Sanjak of Novibazar (see Figure 1 on page 10) and the newly appointed Russian Foreign Minister Alexander Izvolski, reacted violently. Given Russia's weakness his stance was unrealistic to say the least, but he compounded the error by trying to make a deal – an unequal deal which would involve Austria annexing Bosnia and Russia gaining greater access to the Straits of the Bosphorus. Baron Aehrenthal dropped the Sanjak railway but given the revolution in Turkey in July, felt that the annexation of Bosnia would be opportune. The two ministers met on 15 September at Buchláu but nothing was written down, leaving subsequent events open to different interpretation. On 5 October 1908, Austria annexed Bosnia and Bulgaria declared its independence. Both events took Russia by surprise and Alexander Izvolski had made no headway with Britain and France on the Straits question. In any event the Tsar and Peter Stolypin, the Prime Minister, were hardly enthusiastic about handing over the fellow-Slavs of Bosnia to Austria.

The episode only became more of an international incident in 1909. Germany had at first been surprised at developments (it had not been consulted). Given the fact that Austria was now its only friend, it decided to take advantage of Russia's weakness and adopt a more aggressive line. Bülow stated, 'in the present world constellation we must be careful to retain in Austria a true partner'. This was not something Bismarck would have done: 'horse and rider were changing places' (Carr). In January Moltke (the younger) who had succeeded Schlieffen as Chief of Staff told his Austrian equivalent, 'at the same moment Russia mobilises, Germany will mobilise also, and will mobilise her whole army'. This inspired Aerenthal to exploit the victory to the full and he now hoped for war with Serbia; but Russia and Serbia were too weak to respond, while on 21 March Germany presented St Petersburg with a threatening note. The Russians, with intense bitterness, had to give way. 'The crisis was at an end. The Central Powers had won' (M. S. Anderson, *The Eastern Question*, Macmillan, 1967).

This was a cheap victory for the Central Powers and the main consequence of Russia's humiliation was that it was determined not to be humiliated again. Russia embarked on a massive rearmament programme. The events of 1908–9 were for Russia a 'diplomatic Tsushuma' – a reference to Russia's shattering naval defeat at the hands of the Japanese in 1905. Moreover, the events of 1908–9 had made the situation in the Balkans much more volatile – there was little possibility of Austro–Russian cooperation (which had been so important since 1897) and the feeling in Serbia was one of outright hostility. The Serbs were also forced into making a humiliating declaration about good behaviour towards Austria. The Austrian minister in Belgrade reported in April 1909, 'here, all think of revenge, which is only to be carried out with the help of the Russians'.

Why was there no war in 1909?

Basically because Britain and France were unwilling, and Russia unable, to go to war at this time. After its recent defeat at the hands of the Japanese, Russia was so weak it needed to be on good terms with everybody; Izvolski was irresponsible in playing at power politics. From the Austrian point of view it would have actually made sense to have a war with Serbia in 1909 rather than in 1914 by which time the Slav state had doubled in size; and Germany's behaviour merely reflected its anxiety about losing its one ally. Talk soon followed of war with France and Moltke commented that this was probably the most 'propitious' time to fight a continental war. However, all the Germans succeeded in doing with their preponderance of power was insult

Russia and antagonise Britain and France; this was hardly the most intelligent of policies.

And the results? A marked deterioration in the international situation and a victory for brutal diplomacy backed by superior force. There was an increasing polarisation of the powers and an increase in the armaments race to complement the growing naval rivalry between Britain and Germany. Tension had mounted but what happened next would determine whether or not tension would continue to rise or perhaps fall away. Another crisis had passed without war. But there was a limit to how many crises a diplomatic system could actually sustain, without breaking down. Each new crisis brought another possibility of conflict.

Anglo–German naval rivalry (c. 1906–c. 1912)

Although it was recognised that the German naval programme of 1898 and 1900 was aimed at Britain, this did not become a real problem for London until 1905/6. Prior to this, Sir John Fisher, First Sea Lord from 1904, had been quite happy with British naval superiority, though he did begin to move ships from the Mediterranean to home waters. Paradoxically, it was the development by Britain of the 'Dreadnought' (1905–6) – a new type of battlecruiser with a firing range which made all other vessels obsolete – that gave the Germans a chance to catch up. Already in November 1905 Tirpitz had obtained a new naval supplement; now in 1908 he obtained another Navy Bill to build four comparable capital ships a year. This caused great disquiet in Britain and the cry went up, 'we want eight, and we won't wait'. The naval race was on. Tirpitz mistakenly believed that the stronger the German fleet became, the more likely it would be that Britain would come to terms. But as Winston Churchill pointed out, 'whereas the navy was a "luxury" for Germany, it was a "necessity" for Britain': there would be no surrender of naval superiority. At the same time work continued on the development of the small expeditionary force (c. 150,000 men) which could be sent to France to help against Germany – the British Expeditionary Force (BEF).

Theobald von Bethmann Hollweg, the new German Chancellor from 1909, was not a great fan of *Weltpolitik*. He considered the naval race too costly and self defeating; he sought a deal with Britain, but

Tirpitz and the Kaiser held a contrary view and they prevailed. After all, any cutback of the naval programme would be an admission of its failure.

The second Moroccan crisis, 1911

Then in July 1911 another Moroccan crisis blew up. Disorder in Morocco was an opportunity for the French to send in troops. Germany objected, sent a gunboat, the 'Panther', to Agadir and demanded the French Congo as compensation. The French did not panic and were prepared to negotiate a deal. However, the reaction in London was much stronger; German action was seen as yet another attempt to humiliate France and destroy the *Entente* – and it raised fears that Germany might try to claim Agadir as a naval base (something Fisher had warned about during the first crisis in 1905). David Lloyd George, in his famous Mansion House speech on 21 July, issued a firm warning that Britain would prefer war to a pacification at the expense of its honour. In August the fleet was prepared for action and the government agreed 'in principle' that the BEF should be transported to the continent to support France against Germany. In fact, the crisis was settled quite smoothly in November with German recognition of the French protectorate of Morocco in return for a piece of the French Congo. It was, however, another diplomatic defeat for Germany, and Moltke and the military were embittered by the climbdown. Although France was not prepared to go to war over Morocco, the Kaiser personally intervened to insist on a peaceful settlement. It was the British reaction that had taken the Germans by surprise. This proved to be the last gasp of *Weltpolitik*.

The crisis passed and in February 1912 Richard Haldane, Britain's War Minister, visited Germany in an attempt to restore good relations. However, he was unable to get a deal on the naval race; Britain would not agree to neutrality in the event of war, and in any case, Tirpitz wanted a new Navy Bill. Yet the naval race did come to an end the very next month, when the German programme was scaled down considerably. This was because of economic necessity and because the army now demanded the lion's share of resources. Bethmann Hollweg stated in December 1912, 'we have neglected our army and our "naval policy" has created enemies around us'. *Weltpolitik* was at an end;

Figure 3 Cartoon depicting the Agadir crisis of 1911. The Kaiser is shown to be taking a heavy-handed approach.

Weltpolitik had failed. But there had always been more bravado than substance to this policy – in fact it had always been more of an aspiration than an actual policy. Now, however, Germany would turn its attention back to the continent, with unfortunate consequences.

The Naval Race

Dreadnoughts	Great Britain	Germany
1906	1	–
1907	3	–
1908	2	4
1909	2	3
1910	3	1
1911	5	3
1912	3	2
1913	7	3
1914	3	1
Total	29	17

The Eastern Question again: the Balkan Wars 1912–13

One of the results of the French takeover of Morocco was Italy's decision to invade Turkey's remaining North African provinces of Tripoli and Cyrenaica (Libya today) in September 1911. The Italians made heavy weather of their war but it presented the Balkan states with an opportunity to take advantage of Turkey's discomfort. During the course of 1912 an anti-Ottoman Balkan League came into existence: Bulgaria and Serbia signed an agreement in March, Greece joined in May and Montenegro adhered in the autumn.

Austria and Russia were not altogether happy with these developments as they wished to preserve the status quo. They were increasingly frustrated by the fact that they could neither control Balkan nationalism nor benefit from Turkish decay. In October 1912 they issued a joint declaration warning the Balkan League against an attack on Turkey, but this was ignored and war broke out the same month.

Turkey had been wrecked by political turmoil since July and soon succumbed; peace was made with Italy and by November Turkey-in-Europe had all but disappeared. Vital interests of the Great Powers were now in jeopardy and both Austria and Russia were dismayed. In this context Sir Edward Grey stated to the French, 'if either government had grave reason to expect an unprovoked attack by a third power, or something that threatened the general peace, it should immediately discuss with the other whether both governments should act together'. The French now moved their fleet to the Mediterranean, just as Britain had earlier placed its fleet in home waters. In December Haldane warned the Germans that in the event of an Austrian invasion of Serbia, Britain could hardly remain a silent spectator. Haldane added that the existing balance of forces in Europe should be maintained – there could be no defeat of France and no single power could dominate the continent. The Germans were furious at this warning and the infamous Crown Council meeting of 8 December 1912, which discussed the possibility of war (of which more in Chapter 3), should be seen in this context. Subsequently, the Triple Alliance was renewed and Germany assured Austria of its complete support. At the same time the Franco–Russian Alliance was also renewed and extended to cover war with Austria. All these events occurred in December 1912.

Once again war was avoided. In fact, the Great Powers actually cooperated to bring about a settlement, but whether or not this represented a return to concert diplomacy or was just a sham is debatable. A conference of ambassadors met in London early in 1913 to work out a settlement. It seems there was a genuine desire to avoid general war, but events proved difficult to control. War in the Balkans actually resumed in February 1913 but ended in May. At Austria's insistence, an independent Albania was created thus denying Serbia access to the sea.

Then a second Balkan War broke out in July as Bulgaria, feeling isolated and dissatisfied, decided to take on everyone. The outcome in August was a reduced Bulgaria, a partial Turkish recovery and a Serbia that had doubled in size (see Figure 2 on page 26). From the Austrian point of view this was disastrous. However, Austria was not prepared to resort to force without German backing, though it did get the Serbs out of Albania by tough diplomacy in October. There was, in fact, no consensus on Balkan policy between Austria and Germany at this time. Germany was not dissatisfied with the outcome; the king of Greece, a relative of the Kaiser, had done rather well and Germany's ally, Turkey, had made a partial recovery. Nevertheless, growing German influence in the Ottoman Empire was an increasing source of worry to Russia.

As a consequence of this crisis, the powers decided to increase the size of their armed forces. Germany took the lead in January 1913 with an increase in peacetime strength of about 20 per cent to 800,000. In August, France extended the period of service from two years to three and in December Russia decided to add 500,000 to its peacetime strength. Whether increased strength made conflict or conciliation more likely is debatable. Writing about the current state of international affairs in the *Cambridge Modern History* (published in 1910), Stanley Leathes drew comfort from the belief that the piling up of such vast and expensive military forces had done much to prevent war – an argument not dissimilar to apologists of the nuclear deterrent in our own time.

Analysis: 1905–13

So what can we conclude about this period? Because of Russia's defeat at the hands of the Japanese in 1905, there was an imbalance of power in Europe. Moreover, it was an imbalance of which Germany was determined to take advantage. German policy became more aggressive. Equally, Britain was to play a more active role in compensating for this imbalance by supporting the *Entente* powers and by opposing Germany. This led to a restoration of balance at the end of this period, but at the price of polarisation.

In the first Moroccan crisis Germany tried to break the *entente*, but only succeeded in strengthening it. Germany's relative isolation and growing dependence on its one ally, Austria, made it take an aggressive line on behalf of the Habsburgs at Russia's expense over Bosnia in 1909. It was at this time that Moltke made it clear to his Austrian opposite number, Conrad, that any war resulting from Austro–Russian rivalry in the Balkans would have to be fought in accordance with Schlieffen's prescription. If Russia mobilised, France would mobilise too and since 'two mobilised armies like the German and French will not be able to stand side by side without resorting to war … Germany, when it mobilises against Russia, must also reckon on war with France'. Limited war was now an impossibility, in the thinking of the German High Command. This was a dangerous development. But the army did not yet run the government in Berlin; the navy had a louder voice. The naval race with Britain only succeeded in arousing British fears still further and in pushing it closer to the *Entente* powers. Moreover, it was a race the Germans lost and this accounts for its shift away from *Weltpolitik* back to Europe after 1912. The second Moroccan crisis was yet another diplomatic defeat for Germany and the *Entente* was reinforced. By 1913 a balance of power had clearly been re-established (the stalemate of the First World War is testimony to this fact) but as we have stated before, at the price of polarisation.

Why did these crises not lead to war?

For one thing, in both Moroccan crises the Kaiser was pushed into confrontation somewhat reluctantly. He had to be persuaded to send a gunboat to Agadir in 1911. There were other factors too – the German government was not sure of public opinion and because the fleet was not yet ready, it was feared that a British blockade would bring economic chaos. In both 1905 and 1911 the German government created crises, not to cause war, but to win diplomatic victories. However, it did not. By the end of 1911 the Moroccan crisis had been resolved but in France's favour. It cannot be cited as a direct cause of the First World War, although Germany's diplomatic failure engendered immense frustration in Berlin and strengthened the hand of those who favoured the military option.

Similarly, the naval race with Britain cannot be counted as a direct cause of the First World War – it was over by 1912 and in 1914 Anglo–German relations were actually improving. In any case, it did not lead to war in its own right because it was not designed to do so. It was all part of Germany's rather strange bullying approach to diplomacy, whereby Britain was supposed to be threatened into coming to an understanding. Germany's failure in the naval race led to the end of *Weltpolitik* and strengthened the hand of those who favoured a Eurocentric policy based on the development of the army, again with the military solution as very much an option. The Eastern Question, on the other hand, was an issue that had not been resolved.

The 1909 crisis did not lead to war because Russia was too weak and in any case Germany was only looking for a cheap diplomatic victory. However, in the case of both the 1905–6 and 1908–9 crises, it would have made more sense for Germany to resort to war when its position was strong, rather than in 1914 when it was not. The Balkan crisis of 1912–13 did not lead to war because there was a measure of cooperation between the powers (particularly Britain and Germany) and it was not a direct clash between them. Austria was isolated in its dissatisfaction with the outcome, and as the least of the Great Powers it was not in a position to do much about Serbia. There was no Austro–German cooperation on this matter in 1913; without Germany, Austria would not dare fight a war that might provoke Russia. Unlike the Moroccan crises or the Anglo–German naval rivalry, it is not possible to state that the Eastern Question was not a direct cause of the First World War because, as it turned out, it was.

However, we must be careful not to see the characteristics or trends of these years – German diplomatic failure, increasing British suspicion of Germany, growing Austrian concern about Serbia, Russian determination to be armed and ready for the next crisis, and so on – as leading inevitably to a world war. Trends can be changed, sidetracked, reversed as, for instance, improved relations between London and Berlin demonstrated. Yet Europe was divided into two armed camps and there was much talk of war – particularly in Vienna and Berlin. What we have to determine is what was so different about the Balkan crisis of 1914 that it should lead to war, and war on such a scale.

Finally, the obvious point to make about why there was no war between 1905 and 1913 is that no one in authority actually wanted one. Those in government who were advocating a military solution were in a minority or were not ultimately responsible for the decision-making. But their voices were getting louder, and their influence greater.

Essay writing

A few tips

The *purpose* of the essay question is to show that you have mastered the material on a particular topic and are able to support or refute arguments – your own as well as those of the historians you have read.

You must, above all, *address the question* – which can mean clarifying its meaning by defining key terms if there are ambiguities, or answering the question straight away if there are not.

The greatest enemy of the effective essay is *irrelevance*. Anything which interrupts the flow of your argument must be left out (remember you have limited time). However, facts and examples which are related to your argument are as important as the argument itself; those which are not are totally valueless. Do not think that if you simply put every detail down, they will make your case for you. They will not. This narrative approach will only achieve a low grade at best. You must learn to be analytical and refer to the question whenever it is appropriate. It cannot be emphasised too strongly that most Advanced level casualties in history are students who have not mastered the *relevance*.

As far as *style* is concerned you should maintain the pressure of persuasion on the examiner by using short and concise sentences. Remember ABC – <u>a</u>ccuracy, <u>b</u>revity and <u>c</u>larity – are the most important characteristics of style.

A suggested format

You should use the *introduction* to address the question, define its terms and in effect answer it by explaining your view. You should remember that examiners are marking hundreds of A-level essays in a short period of time and they want to know if you know the answer (there can be several 'right' ones but many more 'wrong' ones). They do not want to have to wade through pages of narrative until the question is finally addressed in the conclusion (*'thus in answer to the question we can see that ...'*). You have to get the examiner on your side, right from the start.

If you adopt this approach, the rest of the essay will then justify the position you have taken at the beginning by developing the argument with factual support. By the time you reach the end your *conclusion* should be almost superfluous; you have answered the question and you should have the marks in the bag. You might wish to reiterate your argument or further impress the examiner by pointing forward or looking back, outside the confines of the question, in order to show the breadth of your knowledge.

Some actual essays

(a) **Why did the Great Powers group themselves into a system of alliances before 1914?**

(b) **Why did it prove impossible to solve the problems created by Balkan nationalism before 1914?**

(c) **To what extent was the naval race between Britain and Germany responsible for the First World War?**

Questions (*a*) and (*b*) require you to look at the previous chapter as well as this one; peace and security would seem to be the key to (*a*), but you will need to examine Bismarck's motives as well as those of all the other governments involved – and Britain should not be overlooked. Of course you might want to question the whole idea of an alliance system – after all, few states actually fulfilled their treaty obligations in 1914. As far as (*b*) is concerned, Turkish decay, Great Power rivalry, Balkan rivalry and unfulfilled Balkan aspirations should all feature, but the easiest approach would be to go through the principal crises – Bulgaria 1877–8 and 1885–8, Bosnia 1908–9 and the wars of 1911–13 – to see what unresolved problems were thrown up. Question (*c*) requires you to look at the next chapter as well as this one. If you do decide that the naval rivalry did not cause the war, then you have to state what did.

A documentary exercise

THE AGADIR CRISIS, 1911–1913

Study Documents I, II, III and IV below and then answer questions **1** to **6** which follow:

Document I

It is a question whether we try for naval bases or for a colony, as you wish. The Admiralty is against naval bases, as they divide the fleet.

Kiao-Chau is enough. Your plan of a colony is different, for the fate of colonies will be decided in Europe in the event of war. It will be useful to raise demands in the press and in meetings ... Then I can say, 'I am ready for compromise but public opinion must be considered'. We shall stand firm in Morocco though we may seem to draw back a step ... You may be sure that our Morocco policy will please you. You will be satisfied.

Kiderlin, German Foreign Secretary, in conversation with Class, the Pan-German leader, 1911.

Document II

In a quarter of an hour the bomb explodes. At twelve our ambassadors announce the arrival of <u>the Panther</u> at Agadir. We have caused German firms and business men to send complaints and appeals. <u>We chose Agadir</u> because no French or Spaniards are there. It leads to the Sus, the richest mineral and agricultural part of South Morocco ... We shall take and keep this district as we need a place to settle in.

Zimmermann, Under-Secretary at the German Foreign Ministry, from an official announcement to Class, the Pan-German leader, 1911.

Document III

If we again slink out of this affair with our tail between our legs, if we ·cannot pull ourselves together to present demands which we are prepared to enforce by the sword, then I despair of the future of the German Reich. Then I shall resign.

General von Moltke, the German Chief of Staff, in his diary, 1911.

Document IV

Had I ... allowed the war stage to be reached, we should now be somewhere in France, while the major part of our fleet would lie at the bottom of the North Sea, and Hamburg and Bremen would be blockaded or under bombardment. The German people might then well have asked me why. Why all this for the fictitious sovereignty of the Sultan of Morocco, for a piece of the Sudan or the Congo? ... They would have had every right to string me up from the next tree.

German Chancellor, Bethmann-Hollweg, in a confidential letter to von Weizsädeer, Premier of Württemberg, after the crisis, 1911.

1 In the context of these documents, identify 'the Panther'
   (Document II).   (1)

2 Give one reason why General von Moltke should refer to Germany 'again' slinking 'out of this affair' (Document III). **(2)**

3 Noting the origins and content of Document I, what can a historian learn from this Document about the tactics used by politicians? **(4)**

4 a) To what extent do the authors of Documents I and II agree about the reasons for German involvement in Morocco?

   b) How reliable would you judge each of these documents to be as a source of information about the reasons why 'We chose Agadir' (Document II)? **(7)**

5 To what extent do the authors of Documents I and IV agree as to the risks involved in German action in Morocco? **(4)**

6 Using these documents, and your own knowledge, assess the effects of the Agadir crisis on German foreign policy in the period 1911–1913. **(7)**

ULEAC 1995

CHAPTER THREE

WHO WAS RESPONSIBLE FOR THE OUTBREAK OF WAR IN 1914?

Objectives

◢ To study attitudes in Great Britain, France, Russia, Austria and Germany

◢ To determine who was responsible for the outbreak of war in 1914.

1914
Sarajevo assassinations (28 June)
German 'blank cheque' to Austria–Hungary (5–6 July)
French state visit to Russia (20–23 July)
Austrian ultimatum to Serbia (23 July)
Serb reply; Austria breaks off relations (25 July)
Austria declares war on Serbia (28 July)
Russia orders general mobilisation (30 July)
Germany sends ultimatum to Russia and France (31 July)
Germany declares war on Russia (1 August)
Germany invades Luxemburg and sends ultimatum to Belgium (2 August)
Germany invades Belgium and declares war on France (3 August)
Britain declares war on Germany (4 August)

The events

As 1914 dawned it would be wrong to suggest that tensions were either rising or abating; there were conflicting signs. Anglo–German relations were improving – for instance agreement was reached on the Berlin–Baghdad railway – whereas Russo–German relations were deteriorating. German involvement in the restructuring of the Turkish army brought howls of protest from St Petersburg and the Germans were forced to downgrade their principal military adviser, Liman von Sanders. Also, in January, the Russians inaugurated their Great Military Programme which was due for completion by 1917. This alarmed the Germans because it envisaged a mobilisation time of 18 days which would render the Schlieffen Plan utterly useless. In February 1914 the Kaiser commented: 'Russo–Prussian (i.e. German) relations are dead once and for all. We have become enemies.' And Moltke stated in May 1914 that Germany was now ready for war but by 1917, when Russian rearmament was complete, Germany's strategic position would be hopeless. However, it is clear that he was fatalistic rather than enthusiastic.

Assassination

The main area of trouble remained the Balkans. Here the *Entente* powers were going from strength to strength. The Germans just did not have the money to splash around to retain friendships there, though Berlin did manage a loan to Bulgaria in July. The French, already well established in Belgrade, made an important loan to Greece at the end of 1913, and the Tsar's visit to Rumania in June 1914 was an enormous success. *Entente* success in the Balkans had been helped by the Central Powers' disarray; there was no consensus between Vienna and Berlin and as late as March 1914 the Kaiser declared that Austria would be 'completely crazy' to consider using force against Serbia. Thus, although there was much talk of war in Vienna, all that was practicable was a diplomatic counter-offensive. In the Matscheko Memorandum drawn up on 24 June, Vienna proposed that the best way forward for the Central Powers was not war, but an alliance with Bulgaria and Turkey. No war was planned, but then, on 28 June 1914, the Archduke Franz Ferdinand, heir to the Habsburg throne, and his wife were assassinated by a Serbian terrorist in Sarajevo.

The Archduke's visit to Sarajevo was a catalogue of errors. The day of the visit was Serbia's national day which made it an immense provocation. The royal couple drove around town in an open-top car, an easy target for terrorists for they had no armed guard. Despite this, the terrorists from the Black Hand gang only succeeded in assassinating the couple when the Archduke's driver got lost and turned round in front of one of them, Gavril Princip. He could not miss.

Blank cheque

The next five weeks are of immense importance and you should be very aware of all the dates and details. Too often the 'war-is-inevitable' school of thought sees the outbreak of the war as unavoidable. These last events are for them of little significance, the occasion rather than the cause for war. This would be a wrong approach. What happened in these five weeks was in fact crucial.

Figure 4 The Archduke Franz Ferdinand and his wife about to drive away from the Town Hall in Sarajevo, on that fateful day – 28 June 1914

Clearly the assassination of the heir to the throne by Serbian terrorists was an affront to Habsburg dignity and prestige, and something had to be done about it. At first there was no unanimity – Conrad, the Chief of Staff, urged war; Count Stephen Tisza, the Hungarian Minister-President, was opposed; and Count Berchtold, the Chancellor, hesitated. What tipped the scales was the attitude of Germany. Franz Joseph wrote to the Kaiser requesting support and on 5 July at a critical meeting it was decided to give full support to Vienna, with the assurance that Germany would come to its aid if Russia intervened. It was time to make a clean sweep of the Serbs, declared the Kaiser. On the following morning (6 July) Bethmann Hollweg gave the **'blank cheque'**, telling the Austrian ambassador he could count on German support whatever the decision in Vienna. Still the Austrians dithered.

Ultimatum

Tisza could not be persuaded for a week. When finally, on 14 July, it was decided to send an ultimatum to Serbia, it was discovered that the army was not ready as critical units were on harvest leave! Thus, full advantage was not taken of the moral shock caused by the assassination and it looked as though the crisis might blow over. Then on 23 July Vienna sent Belgrade an **ultimatum** so severe it was bound to be rejected. An acceptance by Serbia would turn it into a virtual police protectorate of the Habsburg Empire.

It was at this point, on 24 July, that Europe woke up to the seriousness of the crisis. The Russians were taken aback by Austria's aggressiveness and it appeared to them that the Central Powers were intent upon an all-out triumph. Russia could not face another humiliation like 1908–9 so it offered Serbia unspecified support, publicly stating that Russia 'could not remain indifferent'. Even so the Tsar's government urged caution and on 25 July Serbia, in a polite but not submissive reply, accepted practically all Austria's requests – but not all. Vienna broke off diplomatic relations and Sir Edward Grey, Britain's Foreign Minister, proposed a four-power conference to defuse the situation, but met with little response from the Central Powers.

War

On 28 July, much to his military advisers' dismay, the Kaiser changed his mind about the crisis (or lost his nerve) and decided that a diplomatic victory would suffice. However, on the same day Austria declared war on Serbia and Russia, fortified by French support, ordered a partial mobilisation of its army – not as a prelude to war but as a gesture of support to Serbia and to exert pressure on the Austrians to think again. On 29 July, Germany ordered Russia to halt its mobilisation. Russia's partial mobilisation, had set off alarm bells in Berlin because of the implications for the Schlieffen Plan; Moltke and von Falkenhayn were urging German mobilisation. To their relief Russia went to full mobilisation on 30 July (the Tsar had been advised partial mobilisation was not feasible) and they were able to blame Russian aggression for their next moves. Germany mobilised on 31 July and declared war on Russia the next day. Because of the Schlieffen Plan, the French were now asked to be neutral. Paris simply replied that it would 'act in accordance with its interests'. On 3 August, Germany declared war on France and invaded Belgium. Ostensibly because of the violation of Belgian neutrality, Britain declared war on Germany on 4 August.

The First World War had begun. As Sir Edward Grey so poignantly put it: 'the lamps are going out all over Europe; we shall not see them lit again in our lifetime'.

In actual fact many felt the war would be short – 'over before the leaves fall', the troops would be 'home by Christmas' – and the outbreak was greeted with relief or even joy by some. In the run-up to the outbreak of war, the absence of any diplomatic activity is indicative of the fact that the Schlieffen Plan robbed the politicians and diplomats of any flexibility; and the Plan also explains why an assassination in the Balkans led to the invasion of ... Belgium! There are some basic facts to consider – France and Russia declared war on no one. Germany declared war on them both. So was article 231 of the Versailles Treaty – the War Guilt clause – correct? Or is it more complex than that? We shall now look at each of the powers in turn.

The major European powers

Great Britain

Britain was concerned to maintain the status quo; Britain did not want war. There was considerable concern at Germany's restless diplomacy; and the Moroccan crises of 1905 and 1911 and the naval rivalry had pushed Britain firmly into the *Entente* camp. The British government had formulated a continental strategy (involving the British Expeditionary Force) from 1907, and had devised a naval strategy of sorts with the French in 1912, but was under no obligation to get involved in any continental struggle. There was no military alliance. However, Britain was concerned about Germany's growing economic power – its increasing industrial might and commercial potential – and there was a feeling that Germany should be kept in its place. It was felt that the *Entente* alignment could do just that.

Yet the increasing tension between 1905 and 1912 passed. Anglo–German relations were actually improving and if we look at the actual crisis of July 1914, it is clear that Britain was neither planning a war nor even certain about what to do in the event of one.

As late as 20 July 1914 Sir Edward Grey stated that he thought the Austro–Serbian quarrel could be resolved peacefully. When after the ultimatum of 23 July this appeared unlikely, Grey talked in terms of a war between Russia, Austria, Germany and France (and not Great Britain), and hoped to mediate. Herbert Asquith, the British Prime Minister, wrote on 25 July that while he thought a continental war increasingly likely, Britain would not be involved. On 26 July King George V stated that 'England [sic] would maintain neutrality in case war broke out between Continental Powers'. This was hardly a country planning and clamouring for war.

However, by 27 July, Grey was saying the opposite to the German ambassador. He now believed the war could not be localised and would therefore affect the balance of power in Europe. He now favoured intervention. Asquith too was now convinced that intervention was necessary, but at the Cabinet meeting of 29 July the rest of the Cabinet was overwhelmingly opposed (the matter of Belgian neutrality cut no ice) and only after Grey's threat of resignation was it 'decided not to decide'. Of course, Belgium was not really the issue; Grey was much more concerned about the fate of France. But he did not want war; he urged the Germans to call off the Austrians and the Cabinet meeting of 1 August went so far as to tell the French ambassador that 'we could not propose to Parliament at this moment to send an expeditionary force to the continent' – despite the implications of the November

1912 exchange when Britain and France agreed to discuss joint action in a crisis. Thus even as late as 1 August 1914, Britain was not going to get involved in the war.

However, with Germany's declaration of war on Russia on that day, the Cabinet meeting of 2 August became crucial. However, the Cabinet fell apart; Asquith and Grey threatened to resign – John Burns, Sir John Simon, John Morley and Lord Beauchamp actually did (though two changed their minds later), while Lloyd George and others took a back seat, thus enabling the 'rump' of Grey and Asquith to make the decisions. Later that day German troops moved into Luxemburg. This helped the interventionists.

A rather revealing telephone conversation later that evening sums up the situation quite well. General Sir John French telephoned some Cabinet members at dinner and asked: 'Can you tell me old chap, whether we are going to be in this war? If so, are we going to put an army on the continent, and, if we are, who is going to command it?' The reply came back (from Lloyd George) that we would be in the war, we would send an army and he would be in command! Quite clearly the last-minute nature of this decision belies any attempt to make a case for Britain causing the war. The role, or rather the absence of role, of the British Commander-in-Chief in the decision-making process also represents a stark contrast to the role played by his German and Austrian counterparts.

Indeed the Cabinet never did make a decision to go to war. As we have stated, the resignations put it in disarray – and it was left to Grey and Asquith to formulate the ultimatum of 3 August to Germany to stop the invasion of Belgium within 24 hours. Germany's failure to do so led to Britain's declaration of war on 4 August. The determination of Grey and Asquith, the support of the Conservatives, and German aggression had made intervention possible. Moreover, going to the defence of 'gallant, little Belgium' was a way of selling the conflict to the population as a whole, though in truth Belgium was the occasion rather than the cause of the war. Just as Britain had gone to war with Louis XIV and Napoleon to prevent one power dominating, so too in 1914 Britain went to war to stop Germany overrunning France and dominating the continent. After all, if Britain had stayed out and

Germany had won, it would have been much more difficult (and much more expensive) to change matters later on.

However, it is quite clear from all the discussion, dithering and disagreement that Britain was very much reacting to events rather than making them. Britain was not a warmonger. The only possible blame that might be levelled at Britain for causing the war is that it did not take a firm enough stance with Germany and Austria to prevent it, by making it clear that Britain would stand by France and Russia. However, Cabinet divisions made such a statement impossible and in any event what must be decided is whether or not an unequivocal statement from Great Britain would have changed policy in either Vienna or Berlin. It seems unlikely that it would have done. Britain then was not to blame.

France

The loss of Alsace-Lorraine to the Germans in 1871 had been a bitter blow, but revenge (*revanchism*) was a low priority. The foreign policy of the Third Republic was cautious and pragmatic, as was the public mood. Germanophobia (dislike of Germany) only revived in the 1900s with the Moroccan crises. In 1905 France was in a weak position – its ally Russia had been defeated by Japan and its new friend Britain was not committed militarily. As we have seen, Germany tried bullying tactics over Morocco but the outcome was to strengthen the *Entente*. Thus, like Britain, France was concerned about Germany's aims and ambitions. The Anglo–German naval rivalry further consolidated the *Entente*, but the second Moroccan crisis of 1911 proved to be the real turning point. German bellicosity over this issue provoked widespread nationalist agitation in France and with the appointment of General Joseph Joffre as Commander-in-Chief in July 1911, and Raymond Poincaré as Prime Minister in January 1912 (President from January 1913), French policy became more assertive.

Joffre realised that France was not in a strong enough position to wage war in 1911 – current strategic plans were inadequate, the army had insufficient numbers and there was no clear military commitment from its ally Russia (and of course no commitment at all from Britain). In Poincaré, Joffre had a kindred spirit. The new premier brought vigorous leadership and a more robust stance on foreign policy. On his visit to Russia in the summer of 1912 he gave the Tsar a firm pledge of support and encouraged increasing French investment in both Russia and the Balkans. He responded to the Royal Navy's fleet realignment (March) by moving the French fleet to the Mediterranean in September 1912 and a series of discussions led to an agreement in November to discuss joint action with Britain in the event of a crisis. In the meantime, Joffre reshaped French strategy from a defensive one to an offensive one. As early as August 1911 he had persuaded the Russians to commit troops to offensive action by day 16 of a general war, and in staff talks in 1912 and 1913 General Zhilinski pledged over 800,000 soldiers for this operation. Joffre presented his new offensive plan – Plan XVII – in April 1913 and in July President Poincaré called for a credit of 500 million francs to extend military service from two years to three (in response to both Plan XVII and Germany's new Army Law). Plan XVII finally became operational in May 1914 and it envisaged a thrust into Lorraine. It did not, however, envisage British support. And no one was envisaging its implementation, except as a response. Hopes of recovering Alsace-Lorraine gave France something worth fighting for but not sufficient reason for war. France wanted to be ready, but France did not want to start a war.

Indeed when the Balkan crisis blew up, the leaders of France were 'literally and metaphorically at sea' (Keiger). Clearly believing that the Sarajevo assassination would be forgotten, on 16 July 1914 Poincaré set sail for Russia to shore up the alliance, on a trip due to last until the end of the month. It is hard to imagine that the leaders of France would undertake such a trip while plotting a major war! Moreover, there is no evidence to suggest any forthcoming war was discussed when Poincaré was in St Petersburg – five days after the visit the Russians were still uncertain of French support. Moreover, between 22 and 28 July when the crisis really erupted, the President and his Premier were out of communication with Paris. This meant that France's principal decision-makers were to a large extent isolated from the diplomacy of the time (and of course Vienna and Berlin were able to take advantage of this).

In Paris the caretaker government did take some precautionary steps, such as recalling units on leave. On 28 July General Joffre – without official government sanction – assured the Russians of France's 'full and active readiness to faithfully execute her responsibilities as an ally'. Yet even at this late hour the gravity of the situation was not appreciated by the French people who were engrossed in a particularly exciting scandal. In March, Henriette Caillaux, the wife of the Finance Minister, had shot and killed the editor of *Le Figaro*, Gaston Calmette, to prevent him publishing her love letters to Caillaux, written while the Finance Minister was married to his first wife. Understandably, the sensational 'not guilty' verdict got twice the coverage of the Balkan crisis.

When Poincaré did return to French soil on 29 July it was probably too late to stop the course of events. To a large extent, France's action could only be reactive, and its policy was mainly defensive, passive and restraining. Moreover, as the British ambassador pointed out, French public opinion was against going to war over Serbia, and Germany believed France was working to restrain Russia. Indeed it was: on 30 July a telegram was despatched to St Petersburg stating that Russia 'should not immediately proceed to any measure which might offer Germany a pretext for a total or partial mobilisation of her forces'. There was, however, a communication problem between St Petersburg and Paris which was not the fault of the French ambassador (as had been thought hitherto) and Russian mobilisation occurred without French knowledge.

By 1 August, Poincaré believed that a general war was inevitable but it remained his aim not to make the mistake of 1870 when France had rushed into war. He would act with restraint, so that France could not be accused of starting the conflict. By these means he believed public opinion (and Britain) would rally to his side. However, Germany had mobilised and Joffre calculated that every 24 hour delay in mobilising French forces was equivalent to a 15–20 kilometre loss of French territory. He had to threaten resignation to get his way. Even so, together with the mobilisation order, Poincaré issued a two-page proclamation stating 'mobilisation is not war'. Now the Germans requested French neutrality (and the surrender of principal fortresses along its eastern frontier as a guarantee of its sincerity!). René Viviani, the Prime Minister, replied that France would act in accordance with its interests.

On the same day (1 August) Germany declared war on Russia. Now France was obliged under the alliance to declare war on Germany, but would not. Still Poincaré showed restraint. He told the Russian ambassador, 'it would be better that we were not obliged to declare it ourselves and that it be declared on us ... a defensive war would raise the whole country'. Moreover, he was still unsure of the British position. On 2 August the Germans invaded Luxemburg and demanded free passage through Belgium. The Belgians refused. Then at 6.30 p.m. on 3 August, on the false pretext that French aeroplanes had bombed Nuremberg, Germany declared war on France. On 4 August the Germans marched into Belgium and Britain became France's ally.

By this point Poincaré had united the country and had waited for the Germans to assume, in his words, 'full responsibility for a horrific war'. As John Keiger put it: 'In August 1914 patriotic feeling was buoyant, but most people did not want war. Opposition to the war was much greater that has often been thought, whether in France or elsewhere, until about a week before it broke out. French decision-makers understood that.'

There is no evidence that France was planning a war. France, like Britain, was reacting to events. France did not cause the war. Again like Britain, France entered the war for negative reasons – to prevent Germany defeating Russia and dominating the continent. Besides, war was declared on France by Germany, not the other way round.

Russia
Russia's defeat in 1905 at the hands of the Japanese was not only a humiliation that left it weak for years to come, it also spelt the end of Russia's Far Eastern ambitions. The agreement with Great Britain in 1907 was one result of Russia's weakness, but the other was, as we have seen, further humiliation over the Balkans in 1908–9. Relations with Germany had been cool since the Kaiser had tried to take advantage of Russian weakness by exploiting the Moroccan issue, but relations with Austria had been reasonably good since the 1890s. All this was now at an end and Russia made a determined effort to ensure that it would never be humiliated again. A massive rearmament programme was under way.

Russian economic growth between 1908 and 1914 was spectacular. This, together with French loans, enabled the Tsarist government not only to reform, re-equip and expand the army but also to rebuild its fleet. Expenditure on defence rose from 608 million roubles in 1908 to 960 million in 1913. In the meantime it was essential for the new Foreign Minister, Sergei Sazonov, to avoid any confrontation.

Accordingly, he attempted a rapprochement with Germany in 1910–11 (the so-called 'Potsdam Agreement') in which Russia dropped its objections to the Berlin–Baghdad railway in return for Germany's agreement not to support Austrian aggression in the Balkans, nor any railway development in Persia. But the outbreak of the second Moroccan crisis 'made it hard for Sazonov to continue to ride two horses simultaneously' (K. Neilson, from K. Wilson (ed.), *Decisions for War*). Russian support for France was lukewarm and when Haldane visited Germany in February 1912, it looked as though the Triple *Entente* might disintegrate. However, the mission failed and Anglo–French relations were patched up. Anglo–Russian relations, on the other hand, were quite cool; but, as we have seen, when Poincaré came to power, France made a great effort to reinvigorate the alliance with Russia, even visiting St Petersburg in August 1912.

Sazonov's foreign policy then underwent another crisis when the first Balkan War broke out in October. Russia and Austria had actually managed a joint declaration in an effort to restrain the Balkan League but it was to no avail. Though the complete victory of the Balkan states was not for Russia the threat it was for Austria, Sazonov was seriously alarmed that the Bulgars might take Constantinople. Control of the Straits was an issue of immense strategic and commercial significance for Russia. At the same time, the Russian Foreign Minister made it clear to the Serbs that Russia would not support Serbian claims to Albania or an outlet on the Adriatic. However, the Minister for War, Vladimir Sukhomilov, and the General Staff took a different line and almost persuaded the Tsar to order partial mobilisation in support of Serbia. At a crucial meeting on 23 November 1912 the Prime Minister and Sazonov were able to persuade the Tsar not to do this. So despite the 'clamouring' of the Russian press on Serbia's behalf, it was reluctantly decided in December that Russia was as yet too weak to stand up to Austria over this issue. This was not exactly a repeat of the Bosnian humiliation since the outcome (a Serbia doubled in size) was more unfavourable to Austria than Russia, but it was a reminder that military weakness always carried with it the prospect of humiliation, and thereby the prospect that Russia would no longer be counted as a great power.

Rearmament went on apace and by 1914, Russia had 11 dreadnought class battleships under construction and a well-equipped peacetime standing army of 1.3 million men, with a projected wartime strength in excess of 5.3 million (Germany's figures were 800,000 and 4.15 million respectively). Indeed by 1914, Russia was spending more on armaments than any other of the major powers, including Germany. That is not all – the Great Military Programme, begun in January 1914 for completion in 1917, was designed to double the artillery, raise the peacetime army to 1.75 million and reduce mobilisation to a mere 18 days (facilitated by French loans for railway construction). Clearly if Russia was not gearing up for war, it was at least determined to be strong enough to face the next diplomatic crisis without having to back down. However, the next crisis came too soon – it came in July 1914.

An earlier lesser crisis over Liman von Sanders, the German general assigned to the Turkish army, was resolved by negotiation. This was thanks largely to the Prime Minister, Vladimir Kokovstov, who restrained those who were impetuous in the military by making the point that Russia was still not ready for war – 'a war at present would be the greatest misfortune that could befall Russia'. Russia would not be ready for war until 1917. However, at the end of January 1914 the Tsar dismissed the Prime Minister; his wise counsel would be missed. Tension seemed to subside and the Imperial family spent April and May of 1914 in the Crimea. When news of the assassination in Sarajevo reached Russia, the Tsar's ambassador in Vienna mistakenly believed Franz Josef would exercise restraint. Although he subsequently became less optimistic as alarming rumours abounded, by mid-July it seemed that they must have been false and the crisis would go away.

Little is known of the actual discussions that took place during Poincaré's exhausting visit to St Petersburg (20–23 July) but the British ambassador did report that Franco–Russian solidarity had been reinforced and that they would take joint action to prevent any Austrian intervention in Serbia, though by this stage this seemed unlikely. The Austrian ultimatum to Serbia when it did come, was like a bolt from the blue and Sazonov, when he learnt of it on 24 July, exclaimed: 'this means war in Europe'. The Russian Foreign Minister perceptively reported to the Tsar that it was such a brutally-worded document it 'could not be complied with'. He also stated that it must have been concocted in agreement with Berlin who wished to start a war to deliberately now because they believed they could win it. Nicholas II, a weak and ineffectual leader, was less perceptive. He failed to appreciate the gravity of the situation and believed Sazonov was exaggerating. At the crucial Council of Ministers meeting on 24 July Sazonov argued that Serbia should not be allowed to be annihilated. Considerations of public and parliamentary opinion counted for something but more important was Russia's national honour and prestige, which were now at stake. Russia could not stand aside. But no commitment was made to actual military action. There was no decision for war. It was decided that if Austria invaded Serbia, Russia would order a partial mobilisation – as a warning to Austria but not as a provocation to Germany.

What happened next is not altogether clear but at a meeting on 25 July it was decided to implement 'The Period Preparatory to War' which put the entire army on alert and triggered a succession of military activities along the German as well as the Austrian frontier. It would appear that the military chiefs were gearing up for war in the full expectation that it would occur. The Tsar and Sazonov, on the other hand, do not appear to have appreciated the significance of these measures. Moreover, Austria was not deterred and on 28 July when news of the declaration of war arrived, Sazonov still favoured partial mobilisation. The General Staff, however, wanted a general mobilisation, maintaining that a partial one was not feasible (whether or not this is true is open to debate). On 29 July the Tsar signed decrees for both partial and general mobilisation but suspended implementation. He worked hard to keep the peace, despatching a personal envoy and telegrams to Kaiser Wilhelm begging him to restrain the Austrians. On receiving a conciliatory reply, he ordered partial mobilisation only. However, on the same day, the German ambassador inferred that Russia should stop mobilisation. This seems to have convinced Sazonov that war was now inevitable. On 30 July the Tsar, not a strong man at the best of times, was faced with a united front from all his political, diplomatic and military advisers who argued that general mobilisation should not be delayed. After being browbeaten for an hour the Tsar reluctantly agreed. In response, the Germans declared war on Russia on the evening of 1 August.

Russia did not want war in 1914 and Russia did not declare war in 1914. Indeed Russia was not going to be ready for war until 1917. However, the Russians did not want to back down again. The military certainly felt more confident in 1914 than it had done in 1912 and was prepared to risk war. Rearmament had gone on apace and French support seemed certain. The other factor that complicated Russian policy at this crucial time was the absence of firm leadership from the Tsar and the chaotic way decisions were made. Still, mobilisation did not mean war – but it did for Germany.

Like Britain and France, Russia was reacting to events rather than making them – reacting to Austria's aggression towards Serbia. However, the question arises, did Russia need to mobilise? Would there have been a war if Russia had not mobilised? Russia cannot be blamed for the war but had the Tsar been given wiser counsel, it might have been avoided. Or would it have just been postponed?

Austria

Austria's main concerns were internal integrity and controlling events in the Balkans. Since 1897 the agreement with Russia had brought stability to the area. It had survived an anti-Austrian coup in Serbia in 1903 and during the Russo–Japanese War, Austria had observed strict neutrality. The agreement was still in existence when the Bosnian crisis broke in 1908. A change of policy occurred after 1906 with the appointment of two individuals who harboured expansionist aims. Conrad von Hötzendorf, the new Chief of Staff, advocated war against Serbia (and others) in 1907, and in 1909, and in 1911, and in 1912 and of course in 1914! He argued that only the use of armed force could prevent the forces of nationalism from pulling the multinational empire apart. Policy, however, was very much in the hands of Count Aerenthal, the Foreign Minister, who advocated a long-term policy of Habsburg domination of the Balkans either by direct or indirect means. His arguments were similar to Conrad's: expansion would provide the unifying force to prevent the Empire's disintegration. However, Aerenthal wanted expansion, not war. 'He was ready to go to the brink

..., but he was not willing to plunge into the abyss' (Fritz Fellner). His policy culminated in the annexation of Bosnia in October 1908 and though this had originally been proposed by Izvolski, the Russian Foreign Minister, the humiliation of Russia and Germany's heavy-handed intervention spelt the end of Austro–Russian relations – 'the entente with Russia was lost beyond recall' (Bridge and Bullen). Thus despite a diplomatic victory and territorial expansion, Austria's position was in fact less secure after 1908. Aerenthal was sensible enough to realise this and he adopted a conservative policy. However, the instability of the Ottoman Empire and Balkan nationalism were not conservative forces, and by 1911 Italy's war with Turkey was threatening to destabilise the entire area. Aerenthal had Conrad dismissed in 1911 (he was advocating war with Italy, Austria's Triple Alliance partner) but the latter returned to office after the former's death in 1912. Aerenthal's successor was Count Berchtold, a man of lesser ability.

Initially, Berchtold put his faith in concert diplomacy and during the first of the Balkan Wars of 1912–13, this seemed to work. There was cooperation in London in December 1912 to establish an independent Albania and prevent Serbia from expanding to the sea, but the Second Balkan War of July 1913 proved to be a frustrating experience for Austria. Berchtold was unable to rally Germany and Italy against Serbia. He was forced to take unilateral action. He had to issue an ultimatum to get Serbia to withdraw its troops from Albania (October 1913). The success of this more forthright approach seemed to suggest that singlehanded action and the threat of military force got results. Berchtold (and Franz Josef) moved closer to Conrad's position.

As 1914 dawned Vienna was becoming increasingly exasperated by the lack of any Triple Alliance policy in the face of a concerted diplomatic offensive in the Balkans by the *Entente* powers, France and Russia. As we have noted before, there was little cooperation and even less understanding between Berlin and Vienna over the issue of Serbia at this stage. As late as March 1914, the Kaiser dismissed Austria's talk of using force against Serbia as 'crazy'.

But what was Austria to do? The elite genuinely believed that the integrity of the multiethnic empire (11 nationalities; 47 per cent of whom were Slav) was seriously threatened by the panslavist ambitions of Serbia. Although we can see with hindsight that this was an exaggerated fear, at the time it seemed very real – after all, Serbia had doubled in size in 1912–13 and the Serbian Prime Minister had talked openly in 1913 of the need to prepare for the next round against Austria. Moreover, behind Serbia stood a revived Russian Empire.

Yet despite Conrad, Austria was not preparing for war in 1914. As we have seen, the 'Matscheko Memorandum' of 24 June advocated a diplomatic counter-offensive in the Balkans by Germany and Austria to secure Bulgaria, Turkey and possibly Rumania for the Central Powers to counter-balance growing *Entente* influence. Then four days later the heir to the Habsburg throne, the Archduke Franz Ferdinand, was assassinated by Serb terrorists. This was an affront to Austrian dignity that Vienna could not overlook. To do nothing would destroy Austrian prestige and credibility in the Balkans once and for all, and hence would spell the end of Austria's great power status; it could well lead to the break-up of the Empire. For many this was now the hour to 'solve the Serbian question'. The conviction was widespread that war against Serbia offered the only chance of securing the continued existence of the state. This was the context in which decisions were made in Vienna in July 1914.

But Vienna was not prepared to risk a war with Serbia that might bring in Russia, without German backing. Indeed it was hoped that German backing might keep Russia out. Thus on 5 July Count Hoyos was despatched to Berlin to secure the Kaiser's support – which he got in full (the 'blank cheque'). On 7 July the Council of Ministers in Vienna decided on war, yet it took an eternity to bring it about. There were objections from Hungary (Count Tisza feared a European war), the army was on leave, the harvest might be upset, and it was felt appropriate to wait until Poincaré had left Russia so that any Franco–Russian response could not be coordinated. The truth is that despite all his talk of war, Conrad and the Austrian army were totally unprepared for offensive action of any kind. Yet it was decided to go ahead with the ultimatum to Serbia and the declaration of war because, as Berchtold so revealingly put it, it is 'not impossible that the Triple *Entente* powers might yet try to achieve a peaceful solution of the conflict unless a clear situation is created by a declaration of war'. This was also a factor in Franz Josef's thinking when he refused to invite the heads of state to attend the Archduke's funeral. He feared they might come to a compromise. Clearly, Austria wanted war in July 1914.

◢ Source

We started the war, not the Germans and even less the Entente – that I know ... I have the distinct impression that the war was decided upon by that circle of younger talented diplomats who formed Berchtold's political council ... I myself was in lively agreement with the basic idea that only a war could save Austria. As the world situation was then, I am also quite sure that, two or three years later, war for Austria's existence would have been forced upon us by Serbia, Rumania and Russia, and under conditions which would make a successful defence far more difficult at that time ... When the existence of the fatherland is at stake, every patriotic statesman, indeed, every patriot, must go to war.

Leopold Baron von Andrian-Werburg writing in December 1918.
Quoted by Fritz Fellner in **Decisions for War** *(UCL Press, 1995).*

These sentiments were echoed by the Emperor Franz Josef the following month when he stated that 'if we must go under, we had better go under decently'. However, by that stage the third Balkan War that Austria had envisaged had escalated into a Europe-wide war.

However, the fact that a European war occurred instead of a planned local Balkan war was not the fault of the Austrian leadership, though it was aware of the possibility and prepared to risk it. While strategic attention in Vienna focused on Serbia, the decision-makers in Berlin had a very different plan of action in front of them. Indeed Kaiser Wilhelm and his generals had little interest in a Balkan war – in fact they had little concern for Austria's interests at all. German military planning developed a momentum of its own. Germany was supposed to support Austria and deter Russia, but instead used the crisis to unleash a Europe-wide war in order to resolve its own perceived difficulties. Wilhelm II's telegram of 31 July to Franz Josef stated: 'I am prepared, in fulfilment of my alliance obligations, to go to war with Russia and France immediately ... In this hard struggle it is of the greatest importance that Austria directs her chief force against Russia and does not split it up by a simultaneous offensive against Serbia.' He went on: 'In this gigantic struggle ... Serbia plays quite a subordinate role.' But Serbia was Austria's main reason for going to war. Throughout July without informing Vienna, Berlin had been taking quite a different road. There is no doubt that Austria bears responsibility for the outbreak of the war; the Austrians were determined to have their Balkan war at any price. The possibility of war with Russia was clearly recognised. Of all the powers, internal considerations seem to have loomed largest in Austria. But of course the very thing the decision-makers sought to prevent, disintegration, they actually brought about. However, it was Germany that escalated the conflict. But why?

Germany

Under Bismarck the new Germany had enjoyed considerable influence in international affairs, but with the accession of Kaiser Wilhelm II this had been lost. The restless ambition and unpredictability of the Kaiser's policies – the New Course, *Weltpolitik* – had created suspicion and unease. Aggressive attempts to take advantage of France in 1905 and 1911, and Russia in 1909 had only succeeded in alienating these powers – as the naval race had done with Britain in the same period. Indeed 'two decades of rudderless statecraft had left the Reich in a precarious position' (Herwig).

By 1912 *Weltpolitik* was in a diplomatic and financial shambles – and it was quietly dropped. Continental aims re-emerged as the priority, reflected in the Army Bills of 1912–13. It was recognised that Germany's fate would be decided in Europe. Defence of the Fatherland against France and Russia became the priority and with this shift, the army leaders, the advocates of a preventive war, had increasing influence in the corridors of power. At the Crown Council Meeting of 8 December 1912 the Kaiser and Moltke urged war with Russia and France immediately ('the sooner the better') but Tirpitz argued it would be better postponed for 18 months when the Kiel Canal would be completed. Moltke agreed that some delay would also be needed for the press to prepare the people for 'a war against Russia'. Two days later, the Kaiser talked to the Swiss ambassador of the unavoidable 'racial war, the war of Slavdom against Germandom'.

In January 1913 a new Army Bill was introduced: Germany's peacetime strength was raised from 663,000 to 761,000, rising to 800,000 in 1914. However, these increases were more than matched by Germany's enemies, Russia and France, engendering increasing pessimism about the future in Berlin. All this armament expenditure had to be justified to the taxpayers and in all the countries, government spokesmen talked of the growing risk of war. Warlike nationalism was perhaps more pronounced in Germany where there was much discussion of the impending biological struggle between Slav and Teuton (an ethnic name for Germans). The Kaiser reiterated his view that a racial war was imminent to English guests at the Crown Prince's wedding in May 1913. And the Kaiser's increasing belligerence was not confined to Slavs – in November 1913 Wilhelm informed King Albert of Belgium that war with France was now 'inevitable and imminent'. Of course it would be naive to take all of the Kaiser's outbursts at face value but they do reflect a certain consistency of thought. Although the elite was concerned about the leftward trend in German politics (by 1912 the Socialists were the largest party in the Reichstag) and many historians, particularly German ones, still stress the importance of domestic pressures, internal factors do not seem to have been important (as they were in Austria). The Russian menace was the principal concern.

After the matter of Liman von Sanders (see pages 62–3), we noted that Wilhelm II commented (in February 1914), 'Russo-Prussian relations are dead once and for all. We have become enemies.' In March a press war developed, with German newspapers warning of the future Russian danger and the Russians responding by declaring that they would not be deflected from their goals. Indeed the real turning point had been the Russian announcement of the Great Military Programme in January as the 5,000 kilometres of new railway would, by 1917, render the Schlieffen Plan redundant. In May 1914 Quartermaster General Count von Waldersee issued a memorandum in which he stated that the *Entente* powers would at some point in the future attack Germany from all sides, but that Germany's 'chances of achieving a speedy victory in a major European war are today still very favourable'. This was a point taken up by Helmuth von Moltke a few days later, as Foreign Secretary von Jagow recalled:

◢ Source

The prospects of the future oppressed [Moltke] heavily. In two or three years Russia would have completed its armaments. The military superiority of our enemies would then be so great that he did not know how he could overcome them. In his opinion there was no alternative to making preventive war in order to defeat the enemy while we still had a chance of victory. The Chief of the General Staff therefore proposed that I should conduct a policy with the aim of provoking war in the near future.

German Foreign Secretary von Jagow, May 1914. *Quoted in* Germany *by John C. G. Röhl in Keith Wilson's **Decisions for War** (UCL Press, 1995).*

This attitude was not confined to the military. Bethmann Hollweg, the Chancellor, told the Austrian ambassador, 'if war must break out, better now than in one or two years' time, when the *Entente* will be stronger'. He also stated, 'the future belongs to Russia. It grows and grows and hangs upon us ever more heavily like a nightmare.' Such was the background to the July crisis in Berlin.

When, a week after the assassination, Count Hoyos arrived at Potsdam on 5 July, Kaiser Wilhelm II advised him that Vienna should take 'war-like action' and that, as he reported, if Russia did intervene 'Germany ... would stand at our side'. And this position was reiterated the following day by Bethmann Hollweg. This was the 'blank cheque', a firm commitment to Austria regardless of the consequences. For most of the crisis the Germans stuck to this line. Indeed it was Bethmann Hollweg, along with von Jagow, who handled the situation while the Kaiser departed for his Baltic cruise (July 6–28). Bethmann Hollweg knew of the substance of Austria's ultimatum and pressed Vienna to deliver it, and subsequently pressed them to declare war. British mediation proposals were forwarded to Vienna with advice not to cooperate. Bethmann Hollweg, it would appear, was willing either for a Balkan success or a continental war – the 'calculated risk'. Moltke, of course, preferred the latter. What is striking is the absence of any attempt at diplomatic activity by Austria or Germany with regard to Russia during this period. The Germans simply waited on the Russian reaction, feeling they could not lose. If Russia backed down, the Central Powers would enjoy a great triumph; if it did not, it could be blamed for the hostilities.

Germany's decision to start a European war, formally made on 31 July, in contrast to the 'blank cheque', followed several days of hesitation and debate. The Kaiser on his return on 28 July clearly lost his nerve and tried to back off; as did Bethmann Hollweg on 29 and 30 July when he made a short-lived effort to restrain Austria. However, by then it was too late as Russian mobilisation plans had set off alarm bells in Berlin.

Incredible as it may seem, the German military only had one plan (see box on page 35) and this severely restricted any room for manoeuvre. Once Russia began to mobilise, Moltke felt he had to put the Schlieffen Plan into operation or the opportunity to win a two-front war would be lost – for every hour of delay reduced Germany's chance of dealing a knockout blow in the West. France must be attacked whatever the original cause of the war. Accordingly, on 30 July he telegraphed Conrad, urging him to mobilise against Russia and saying Germany would do likewise. Bethmann Hollweg called off his initiative and was persuaded by Moltke and General von Falkenhayn on 31 July to declare a military emergency and order mobilisation. Russia refused to abandon its mobilisation so Germany was able to persuade its population of the necessity for a 'defensive war'. On 1 August, Germany declared war on Russia. In accordance with the Schlieffen Plan, Germany moved into Luxemburg and delivered an ultimatum to Belgium demanding free passage for its troops on 2 August. Belgium refused. On 3 August, Germany declared war on France (having failed to obtain a declaration of neutrality) and its troops moved into Belgium. On 4 August, Britain declared war on Germany.

'Responsibility for the catastrophe lay principally not with France, or Britain or Russia, but with a small handful of men in Vienna and Berlin' (Röhl). Thus Franz Josef, Wilhelm II, Bethmann Hollweg and Gottlieb von Jagow, Conrad and Berchtold, Moltke and von Falkenhayn were all willing to gamble on a full-scale European war in the summer of 1914. There is no doubt that Austria would have preferred a localised Balkan conflict but the German military believed that a continental war was inevitable and the sooner the better. However, Berlin did not go to war in 1914 in a 'bid for world power' (though it was an opportunity for expansion and a policy advocated by many in the military *Junker* class), nor as a result of the meeting of December 1912. Indeed, Germany was not all that well prepared for war in 1914, but the leaders in Berlin believed the German army was in better shape than either the French or the Russians and saw war as the only solution to 'encirclement'. They also saw the present moment as the best opportunity to halt a deteriorating military balance, to prevent a future in which the *Entente* powers reigned supreme – in which the Slav enveloped the Teuton. Thus decision-making was largely emotional; it came from a pessimistic mental attitude rather than as a result of coherent strategic planning. And much of the responsibility for this rests with Helmuth von Moltke. 'His mind was beset with pessimism bordering on paranoia' (Herwig) but his belief that 1914 was the right moment was in fact completely wrong! He underestimated the *Entente* armies and overestimated his own. The moment had passed; there was already a balance of power.

It would appear then that Article 231 of the Treaty of Versailles, the War Guilt Clause, was about right: Germany caused the First World War. And the 'men of 1914' had no illusions about this. In February 1915, Bethmann Hollweg confessed that the responsibility for unleashing the war depressed him – 'the thought never leaves me, I live with it constantly'. In June of the same year, Moltke, nine months after his dismissal, complained: 'it is dreadful to be condemned to inactivity in this war *which I prepared and initiated*'. Later in the war von Jagow confessed he could not sleep because he knew that Germany 'had wanted the war' which had turned into a catastrophe. So why then are so many textbooks ambiguous about responsibility for the war? The answer lies in the subsequent cover-up by the Germans and the development of a rather facile historiography that found it easier to plump for shared responsibility rather than apportion blame (see next chapter).

TASKS

Discussion

Who was responsible for the outbreak of the war?

Designate five individuals or five pairs to state the case against each of the powers.

Although this chapter has been quite categorical about blame, good cases can still be made against the other powers. After all, they all had reasons for going to war – France wished to recover Alsace-Lorraine, Britain wished to keep Germany in its place, and Russia was not prepared to allow Serbia to be pushed around.

This would be a good exercise for would-be lawyers!

Documentary exercise

GERMAN MILITARY PLANNING

Study Documents A, B, C and D below and then answer questions **1** to **6** which follow:

Document A

If ... war should break out, ... then no end to it can be foreseen; for the strongest and best equipped powers in the world will be taking part in it. None of these powers can be crushed in a single campaign, ... and woe to him that sets fire to Europe.

The elder von Moltke, in a speech to the Reichstag, 1890.

Document B

King Leopold still owed His Majesty a reply to the question submitted to him in January, as to what attitude he, the King, intended to adopt in case an armed conflict should break out between Germany and France or Germany and England. In explanation, His Majesty told me in this connection that he had categorically demanded of the King, during a lengthy conversation in January of this year, that he, the King, should give him a written declaration now, in time of peace, to the effect that, in the case of conflict, Belgium would take her stand on our side, and that to this end the King should amongst other things guarantee to us the use of

Belgian railways and fortified places. If the King of the Belgians did not do so, ... the Kaiser would not be able to give a guarantee for either his territory or the dynasty.

Kaiser Wilhelm II in conversation with the first secretary of the Brussels Legation, 1904.

Document C

However awkward it may be, the advance through Belgium must therefore take place without the violation of Dutch territory. This will hardly be possible unless <u>Liège</u> is in our hands. The fortress must therefore be taken at once (i.e. at the very beginning of mobilisation) ... Everything depends on meticulous preparation and surprise. The enterprise is only possible if the attack is made at once before the areas between the forts are fortified. It must therefore be taken by standing troops immediately war is declared ... the possession of <u>Liège</u> is the *sine qua non** of our advance.

The younger von Moltke, Chief of the General Staff, in a memorandum of 1911.

Document D

Nearly three weeks before the main shock of the armies could begin ... ·six German brigades must storm <u>Liège</u>. It was this factor that destroyed all chance that the armies might mobilise and remain guarding their frontiers while under their shield conferences sought a path to peace. The German plan was of such a character that the most irrevocable steps of actual war, including the <u>violation of neutral territory</u>, must be taken at the first moment of mobilisation. <u>Mobilisation therefore spelt war</u>. None of the Governments except the German and French, and none of the Sovereigns, seem to have <u>understood</u> this.

Winston Churchill, writing in 1931.

1 In the context of these Documents, explain the meaning of
    'violation of neutral territory' (Document D).   **(1)**

2 In the context of these Documents, explain why the capture of
    'Liège' (Document C) was considered important to German
    military planning.   **(2)**

*sine quo no*n: essential condition

3 What can you deduce from Document B about the character of Kaiser Wilhelm II? **(3)**

4 Churchill stated in Document D that 'mobilisation therefore spelt war'. To what extent does the evidence of Documents A, B and C support Churchill's assertion that this was not generally 'understood' (Document D)? **(6)**

5 In the light of the origins and content of Documents B and D, what are the advantages, and possible disadvantages, of these Documents to a historian of German military planning? **(6)**

6 Using your own knowledge, to what extent do these Documents suggest that German military planning made it impossible for Germany to accept a peaceful solution to the diplomatic crisis of July 1914? **(7)**

ULEAC 1996

CHAPTER FOUR

THE GREAT DEBATE: THE HISTORIANS' VERDICT

The great cover-up

Immediately after the war there was no confusion about where responsibility lay. In Article 231 of the Treaty of Versailles, the 'War-Guilt Clause', the victorious allies claimed that war had been 'imposed upon them by the aggression of Germany and her allies', and because of this, reparations were to be exacted in payment for all the damage. In an effort to get the reparations reduced or dropped the German government responded with an orchestrated campaign to prove their innocence which amounted to nothing less than a great cover-up. Between 1922 and 1927 the foreign ministry published 40 volumes of diplomatic documents; and throughout the 1920s the German government subsidised books and journals all of which were designed to reverse the verdict of Versailles. At the same time a tradition of 'patriotic self-censorship' led many historians to cooperate in the plot. Inconvenient 'facts' such as the Schlieffen Plan or the 'blank cheque' were overlooked or omitted and carefully selected anthologies of documents were issued which were designed to shift the responsibility to Russia. It was alleged that Germany had not wanted war in 1914 but had simply been defending itself against the aggressive encirclement of the Triple Entente; Russia and France on the other hand had wanted war; Russia had wanted to expand to the Mediterranean and France had wanted to take back Alsace-Lorraine. Remarkably the German case began to gain acceptance outside Germany and while it was never fully accepted, it did cause others to look again at the war's origins. This in turn led to a shift from allotting responsibility to a search for the underlying long-term causes, and then to the idea of collective responsibility or shared guilt.

Everyone to blame

In 1927 the British historian, G. P. Gooch, argued that all the states had good reasons for going to war in 1914. If this was the case then the question of guilt became meaningless. Attention turned to general causes. Socialist historians argued that the war was a product of capitalism, a search for markets, and thus imperialism was the cause of the war. Others cited the alliance system which turned a local conflict into a continent-wide conflagration; yet others blamed the arms race. Taken together with the repeated crises from 1905, all these factors could be rolled into one general interpretation which condemned (and blamed) the nature of international relations in the pre-war period (cf. *The International Anarchy* by G. Lowes Dickinson published in 1926) which made a breakdown very likely.

Thus by the 1930s a consensus seemed to emerge suggesting that all the powers had somehow been responsible – summed up in the words of the wartime British Prime Minister, David Lloyd George, in his memoirs: 'the nations slithered over the brink into the boiling cauldron of war'. Even after the Second World War, a committee of French and German historians agreed (in 1951) that 'the documents do not permit attributing a premeditated desire for a European war on the part of any government or people in 1914'. However, by this stage, things were already beginning to change.

During the war Luigi Albertini wrote a three-volume work (not published in English until 1952–7) which refocused on the 'blank cheque' and the Schlieffen Plan, as did A. J. P. Taylor in his 1954 publication, *The Struggle for the Mastery in Europe 1848–1914*, though his was a long perspective. Interestingly, the Schlieffen Plan itself was not published in full until Gerhard Ritter's work of the same name came out in 1956 (in English in 1958). Appropriately though it was a German, Fritz Fischer, who really stirred things up in 1961 with his seminal work, *Griff nach der Weltmacht* (literally, *Grasp for World Power*) which was published in English in 1967 under the more innocuous title, *Germany's Aims in the First World War*.

The Fischer thesis

Fischer's book was concerned with Germany's aims during the war, rather than its origins. In particular, he discovered a remarkable memorandum (the 'September Programme') by the German Chancellor, Bethmann Hollweg, dated 9 September 1914, setting out Germany's aims for the domination of Europe which included the annexation of

Belgium, Poland and the Baltic states, as well as a worldwide system of naval bases, a colonial empire in Central Africa and a European Customs Union (*Mitteleuropa*). In addition, in the introductory section of the book Fischer contended that Germany bore a large part of the responsibility for the war – the first time a German had said this – because the German ruling elite harboured expansionist aims and believed that a successful war would consolidate the established order at home.

Fischer's book caused a sensation, particularly in West Germany, and thus reopened the war guilt issue. He followed it up in 1969 with *Krieg der Illusionen* (*War of Illusions*, 1975) which focused on the years 1911–14. Now, instead of ascribing Germany a large share of the responsibility, he went further and argued that Sarajevo was seized on by Germany as a pretext to launch a preplanned continental offensive (and he assigned great significance to the 'War Council' of 8 December 1912 to support this point). Again he emphasised the importance of internal issues in foreign policy decisions – in particular the ruling group's fear of socialism. The old orthodoxy of collective responsibility was thus overturned; but what has replaced it?

After Fischer

Between the wars historians had to rely on collections of documents published by governments and the memoirs of the statesmen involved, neither of which were fully reliable. As we have seen, the Germans were the first to publish their documents but the Austrians, French, British, Russians and Italians all followed suit, if only to show that they had nothing to hide. Since 1945 the European archives have been opened up to the public – Fischer had access to the Imperial Archives at Potsdam – and historians have been able to compare what was published with what was 'overlooked'. In addition, they can now turn to private letters and diaries and many other sources. In short, there is now a greater amount of evidence than there ever was. So where does that leave us? Is there a new orthodoxy?

New research has confirmed that Britain, France and Russia did not want war in 1914, but they were ultimately willing to fight rather than allow their allies to be beaten. New research has also confirmed that the Austrians were determined to use force against Serbia and they saw little chance of avoiding war with Russia. What of Germany? Writing in 1983 Norman Stone stated, 'not many historians nowadays dissent from the proposition that the German government, egged on by its generals, deliberately provoked the war of 1914'; James Joll in 1984 agreed in his book, *The Origins of the First World War*, that by December 1912 the German leaders saw 'war as inevitable'. Hartmut Pogge von Strandmann writing in 1988 stated, 'all the available evidence states that it was mainly Germany which pushed for war and that without the German drive to extend her hegemony a major war would not have started in Europe in 1914'. And in 1995 John Röhl wrote in his essay 'Germany':

German policy in the crisis of July 1914 must rank as one of the great disasters of world history. The leaders of arguably the most successful country in Europe ... took decisions which plunged it and the other powers into a ghastly war ... any German with inside information on how the war had really begun knew that the responsibility for the catastrophe lay principally not with France, or Russia, or Britain, but with a small handful of men in Vienna and Berlin.

And in 1997 Holger Herwig concurred: 'the leaders in Berlin ... saw war as the only solution'. So 80 years on from the Treaty of Versailles, it would appear that Article 231 was about right: Germany caused the First World War.

However, while we can be certain that Germany started the war, determining quite why and when Germany decided to go to war is a far more complex matter – principally because German policy-making was neither systematic nor coordinated. Thus, while we can state quite firmly that Moltke wanted a continental war, we can also state that the Kaiser dithered and the Chancellor gambled. It is not that clear cut.

So, has subsequent research left the Fischer thesis intact? Not really. Germany went to war in 1914 not in a bid for world power but because of growing feelings of insecurity and pessimism. World power would not have been an unwelcome outcome but Bethmann Hollweg's expansionist September Programme should be viewed in the context of what he thought was imminent victory. Did the German government plan a war in December 1912? This seems unlikely too – no subsequent plans have been uncovered and little was done in a systematic fashion to build up the army and its supplies for such an event. The army remained at 800,000 and ammunition reserves were 20–50 per cent short of required levels in 1914. Indeed, it could be argued that nothing was done in a systematic fashion in Wilhelmine Germany. The decision for war was not taken in 1912; it was taken in 1914. And what of the primacy of internal factors? This is also unlikely. Those who took the decisions in Berlin were more concerned with the growth of Russian power and with a desire for a decisive racial clash between Teuton and Slav. They wrote about encirclement, fear of losing great power status, of being enveloped by Russian hordes and so on – not of any fear of being ruled by German socialists. The decision-makers in Berlin responded emotionally rather than rationally to the crisis of 1914. That is why they picked the wrong moment and lost. They simply took a leap in the dark.

Conclusion – and some other issues

War guilt is a relatively new concept – after all, until the twentieth century war had always been seen as an acceptable means of policy. But the problem with the 1914–18 war was that it turned out to be a catastrophe, with unprecedented loss of life. Because of this we have sought to ascribe blame and we have concluded that such a momentous event must have had deep-rooted causes. However, as was suggested at the beginning of Part 1, this might be the wrong way to look at it. In 1914, no government realised that it was embarking on a four-year struggle – for many the phrase 'over by Christmas' was a firm belief rather than a wish. It was felt modern technology would be decisive and that in any case states would not be able to afford to sustain warfare on such a grand scale for any length of time. If, then, we are simply looking at another short limited war, like the Franco–Prussian War of 1870–71 or the Russo–Japanese War of 1904–5, do we need to consider the long term? And is guilt appropriate?

The answer is no and yes. To take the matter of causation first, it does seem that many of the alleged long-term causes simply do not stand up under close examination. Take for instance the idea put forward (by Lenin among others) that the war was *a capitalist and imperialist conflict for markets*. The main imperial conflicts seem to have been between Britain and France, and Britain and Russia, and these had been resolved by the *Ententes* well before 1914. And did the Austrians really covet the Balkans for its wealth? Businessmen were divided on the desirability of war – it depended upon one's business. Overseas trade would be badly hit but arms manufacture would benefit. What of the *arms races*? The Anglo–German naval rivalry was over by 1914 but the other races clearly did have a bearing though Austria, Serbia and Russia had not been engaged in an arms race with each other. What of the *alliance system*? Britain was not in an alliance and yet went to war. Italy was part of the Triple Alliance but belatedly joined the other side. Germany was not obliged to give a 'blank cheque'. Russia did not have an alliance with Serbia. Moreover, when Germany declared war on Russia, France should have declared war on Germany but did not. Again the matter is not clear cut, though it is true to say that there were two rival blocs arming to the teeth, and that this was not a healthy situation. Moreover, it is true that once war broke out, many underlying causes did become issues in the war – fleets, empires, security and status were all at stake, and long-held ambitions came to the fore as war aims.

As far as *guilt* is concerned, it is right that historians should apportion responsibility and given that the deaths of so many were unnecessary (what did the war achieve?), making a value judgement about those responsible is not an unreasonable thing to do. After all, this idea that no one knew the war was going to be a catastrophe is becoming less tenable. Any military man who had the slightest knowledge of the American Civil War (1861–5) with its Gatling guns, trench warfare and enormous carnage, must have had at least a slight premonition that this was the shape of things to come. It is clear that Moltke the elder did, when he addressed the Reichstag in 1890 at the ripe old age of 90. Walter Goerlitz summarises:

◢ Source

If that war should break out which hung like a **sword of Damocles** *over the head of the German nation, then no end to it could be foreseen; for the strongest and best equipped powers in the world would be taking part in it. None of these powers could be completely crushed in a single campaign ...'And woe to him that sets fire to Europe.'*

Walter Goerlitz summarising Moltke's address. Quoted in
The Significance of the Schlieffen Plan *by L. C. F. Turner*
from the **Australian Journal of Politics and History**, *vol. XIII, no.1 (1967).*

KEY TERM

The **sword of Damocles** refers to an imminent danger which may at any moment descend upon a person or people. It is based on a story from Ancient Greek Sicily when a sword was suspended by a hair over the head of a flatterer named Damocles at the court of Dionysus of Syracuse to impress upon him how precarious happiness was!

It is ironic that the man who set fire to Europe was probably Moltke's nephew. But Moltke the younger also had no illusion about a short war – he hoped for a quick campaign in the West but he realised that the battle in the East would be another Armageddon. As early as 1905 he predicted that the next war would be a 'long and tedious struggle' which would leave even a victorious Germany 'utterly exhausted'. Again in 1912 and 1914 he repeated his belief that it would be a protracted struggle.

Peter Durnovo of the Russian State Council warned Tsar Nicholas II that the next war would be a terrible conflict which would bring down the existing order. And what did Sir Edward Grey mean when he stated that the lights were going out all over Europe and would not be lit again in his lifetime? Many realised that they were standing on the edge of a precipice. A war that involved all the major powers was not going to be any ordinary war.

What of the mental assumptions of the decision-makers of 1914? This is more difficult to assess but we cannot discount the influence of Charles Darwin and the idea of the struggle for survival. Conrad insisted war was natural and both Bethmann Hollweg and Moltke talked of moral regeneration and a new age brought about by war. Then there are also the concepts of honour and national pride, and the belief in the false idea of historical inevitability – a war was bound to come – a mistake common to both German generals and history students alike! All of these must have played a part but their exact measurement is impossible.

Many of the reasons for going to war in 1914 were either misconceived or plainly mistaken. Was the integrity of the Austrian Empire really threatened by Serbia? This was the basic assumption that underlay the outbreak of the war, but was it valid? The Habsburg Empire held together rather well for many years during the war under difficult conditions – which rather contradicts the idea that it was on the verge of collapse. Our recent experience of events in the old Yugoslavia somewhat undermines the idea that the peoples of the Balkans are bound together by the brotherhood of panslavism. One thing is for sure though, going to war and losing did make Austria collapse. And did Russia really need to mobilise in support of Serbia? Serbia was in fact quite strong and able to look after itself, as the early campaigns demonstrated. And was Germany really surrounded by hostile powers who were about to attack? The answer is no.

Were the Germans right to fear Russian power in the future? Clearly the Soviet Union later realised this sort of potential, but the German government consistently overestimated the power of Tsarist Russia, while at the same time making the big mistake of underestimating France. After all, the Germans beat the Russians but they could not beat the French. Indeed, this whole idea of the 'sooner the better', that the time was right and that Germany could win today but not tomorrow was wholly wrong. Germany's moment had passed. There was already a balance of power; it would have made more sense to fight in the 1890s, or 1905, or 1909 – but not in 1914.

So was the war pointless? It does seem that the decision-makers in Vienna and Berlin got it all wrong – but at least the outcome was that people were now no longer to be ruled by Habsburgs and Hohenzollerns (the Prussian royal family) and their generals, and that was perhaps some improvement in the long term, though not in the short run – since for many the experience had to be repeated over again, arguably because the side that lost in 1918 simply could not accept that defeat.

Quite why the First World War did go on so long, and quite why Germany did lose, is the subject of the final chapter.

Notemaking

A few tips

As you are probably aware, notemaking is the *foundation* of all your study activity. The notes you make act as a shorthand to remind you about what you have read and they also (often) form the basis for essay writing and (usually) for revision. Moreover, notemaking makes reading *an active process* as you are required to concentrate and extract the most important points.

The two most common errors when notemaking are either to write out too much – there is no point in writing out practically the whole book – or too little – thereby missing out important points. Proper notemaking requires you to think hard about what is relevant and this can be quite difficult when you are unfamiliar with a topic.

It is best to read through a chapter in its entirety first, to put the content in perspective – rather than make notes as you go along.

Another useful tip is to ensure that your notes are *easy on the eye*. A densely packed set of words is rather off-putting when it is time for revision. It is important to space out your notes and break up the pages with gaps (these can be useful for extra points later). Always indent, and use headings, subheadings, numbered points, underlining, colours, etc.

Above all, make your notes interesting. Notemaking is a personal matter and you should end up with an approach that best suits you.

Making notes on this chapter

This chapter already has a number of headings, though the second half does not. Here are some guidelines:

1 The great cover-up

2 Everyone to blame

3 The Fischer thesis

4 After Fischer

5 Conclusion and some other issues

   (a) Causes

      (i) imperialism

      (ii) arms race

      (iii) alliance system

   (b) Guilt – a long war?

   (c) Misconceived reasons

CHAPTER FIVE

POSTSCRIPT: THE GREAT WAR 1914–18

Objectives
◢ To examine why the First World War lasted so long
◢ To investigate why Germany lost the war.

1914   War begins (August)

Germany invades Luxemburg, Belgium and France

Russia invades Germany and is defeated at Tannenberg (26–30 August)

Battle of the Marne (5–10 September)

Battle of the Masurian Lakes (6–15 September)

Germans retreat in West to the River Aisne and dig in 'Race to the Sea' (October–December)

First Battle of Ypres (18 October–22 November)

Turkey declares war (14 November)

1915   Second Battle of Ypres – gas used (22 April–27 May)

Allies land in Gallipoli (25 April)

Russians retreat in face of German advance (May)

Italy enters war on *Entente* side (23 May)

Serbian army collapses (7 October)

Allies evacuate Gallipoli (December–9 January)

1916   Battle of Verdun (21 February–18 December)

Brusilov offensive (4 June–20 September)

Battle of the Somme (1 July–18 November)

Rumania joins allied side (27 August)

Rumania defeated (December)

1917   Germans announce unrestricted submarine warfare (31 January)

Germans shorten the line in the West (23 February–5 April)

Tsar Nicholas II abdicates (12 March)

USA enters the war (6 April)
Nivelle offensive (19–29 April)
Battle of Passchendaele (31 July–10 November)
Battle of Caporetto (24 October–12 November)
Bolsheviks seize power in Russia (7 November)
Battle of Cambrai (20 November–8 December)

1918 Wilson's '14 points' (8 January)
Treaty of Brest Litovsk (3 March)
German offensive (21 March–18 July)
Allied counter-offensive (18 July–10 November)
Bulgaria capitulates (29 September)
Mutiny of German sailors at Kiel (28 October)
Turkey capitulates (31 October)
Austria capitulates (3 November)
German Republic proclaimed (9 November)
Kaiser flees to Holland (10 November)
Germany capitulates (11 November)

Introduction

Why did the First World War last so long and why did Germany lose? The two questions are of course interrelated. The war lasted so long because Germany failed to achieve a quick victory – and Germany lost for largely the same reason.

The Central Powers – Austria and Germany – needed a quick victory in 1914 because they were outnumbered; they could not win a war of attrition if the *Entente* powers stuck together. The Germans believed that their superior army would enable them to deliver a knockout blow; however, modern weaponry, especially the machine gun, was a great equaliser, a great leveller in both senses of the word. Failure in 1914 led to a stalemate – there was a military stalemate brought about by comparable technology and resources, a political stalemate because the alliances held and a diplomatic stalemate as no one was willing to compromise.

German success on the Eastern Front led to another opportunity in 1918, but the arrival of US troops on the *Entente* side nullified any German advantage. Failure of the offensive in 1918 brought defeat.

Why did the Germans fail in 1914?

The events

First of all, the Germans met unexpectedly strong resistance from the Belgians, both in military terms and in terms of the destruction of infrastructure. Railway lines and bridges could be replaced but the destruction of railway tunnels caused considerable hold-ups. Soon the Schlieffen Plan was falling behind schedule though Liège was taken only two days late. The delays enabled the BEF to land and play a part in delaying the Germans at Mons and Le Cateau.

At the same time, the French Plan XVII (the advance into Lorraine) failed at the cost of 300,000 casualties (Joffre sacked 140 generals); however, Joffre did not lose his nerve and he now had a clear idea of how to deal with the real German advance, which he might not have done had he been allowed to advance into Lorraine as in Schlieffen's original plan.

On 25 August Moltke mistakenly sent two corps (about 60,000 troops) to the Eastern Front to deal with the unexpected Russian invasion – given that he also had to leave two corps to deal with the Belgian army, his crucial right wing was now reduced from 16 to 11 corps.

The last day of August proved critical as the French halted the German Second Army (led by von Bülow) at Guise and Kluck wheeled south-east to assist (2 September), thereby changing the direction of his advance to the east rather than the west of Paris (see Figure 5 on page 102). The capital could not now be encircled. The shortage of men was forcing all the German armies to close up on each other, in any case. By the time the Germans reached the Marne they were exhausted, having marched a considerable distance from their

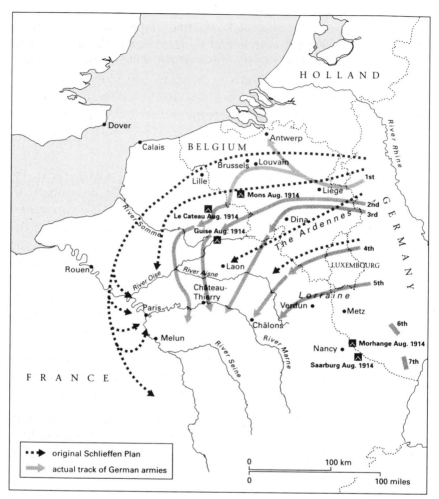

Figure 5 The German attack, 1914

railheads. They were short of supplies and had only six days left in which to win and then turn east!

Their right wing was now exposed to a flanking attack from the direction of Paris. The French counter-attack – the Battle of the Marne – began on 5 September. A gap appeared between Army Groups 1 and 2 and the BEF stumbled into it. All was confusion – it would appear that at this decisive moment when a decision had to be made, there was no communication between Army Groups 1 and 2 and Moltke for four days (5–9 September). Eventually, Moltke empowered a deputy to make the appropriate decisions and he (Lieutenant Colonel Richard Hentsch) ordered a retreat to the Aisne which Moltke later confirmed. However, by now the latter was a broken man, believing the war to be lost and he was quietly replaced on 14 September. Whether or not the Germans needed to retreat at this point has been debated ever since. Nevertheless, the great gamble had failed and there existed no fallback plan.

Therefore von Falkenhayn tried to resurrect the Schlieffen Plan. He reinforced the right and decided on an outflanking movement. In what has been inaccurately termed the 'race to the sea', the two armies tried unsuccessfully to turn the flank of the other before halting at the English Channel. This second failure shook Falkenhayn and he informed the Kaiser on 13 November that the army was exhausted and that the campaign in the West had probably been lost. He stated: 'As long as Russia, France, and England hold together, it will be impossible to beat them.' Chancellor Bethmann Hollweg, however, refused to contemplate defeat at this early stage and the war went on.

The soldiers dug in to avoid the murderous fire of the machine gun and soon a line of trenches 765 kilometres long ran from Flanders to Switzerland. Static trench warfare had begun. It was a stalemate.

In the East, the Russians had sprung a surprise by going on the offensive. They were eventually defeated at the Battles of Tannenberg (August) and Masurian Lakes (September) and were thrown back out of Germany.

Analysis

The first point to make is that the Schlieffen Plan had not failed; it had not been applied. The plan that was applied should more appropriately be termed the Schlieffen–Moltke Plan (David Stevenson, *The Outbreak of the First World War*, Macmillan, 1997) because of the crucial changes Moltke had made to it.

It had serious flaws. Too few soldiers were on the right wing and too many were on the left. Thus Moltke did not have numerical superiority in the crucial areas where he needed it. Moreover, he could not organise adequate supplies (he relied on horses rather than lorries) and he took soldiers out of the attack to deal with the unexpected Russian advance. In addition, once the advance began to unravel near Paris and Army Groups 1 and 2 lost touch with each other, Moltke himself went to pieces and sanctioned a retreat which may not have been necessary.

In sharp contrast, Joffre showed stoic courage in the face of adversity. It remains to be said that the Allies were not easily defeated – the Belgians offered unexpected resistance, the BEF fought valiantly and the French army was much better organised than in 1870. Moreover, the machine gun greatly facilitated a defensive posture (the cavalry was the first casualty). The two sides were in fact pretty evenly matched. This is why it became a long war.

Why was there no military resolution in 1915–17?

As we have noted, the opposing lines of armies dug in and the separate lengths of trench began to link up in an elaborate system of dugouts, reserve lines, barbed wire entanglements, machine-gun posts, communication lines etc. that were as much as six kilometres deep in places. All this combined to give defence a considerable advantage over attack – it has been estimated that the attackers lost at least one-third more in casualties than the defenders. No one came up with a way of overcoming this impasse. It is all very well writing about lions led by donkeys but no one on either side knew how to break the deadlock. Here was a war in which the horse was redundant (an easy target for the machine guns and expensive to feed) and in which the internal combustion engine had yet to come of age – engines could not propel much armour and when they did, they were unreliable.

Many methods were tried: massed artillery, but this only served to churn up the ground and forewarn of an attack; poison gas, but this was only really effective the first time and its efficacy took the Germans by surprise (as did the change in the direction of the wind!); tanks were used by the Allies with some success at Cambrai in November 1917, but in reality they were unreliable and were only a success in the last months of the war.

There was no alternative to attrition though this is not to absolve the generals from all responsibility – they were usually too far from the front to appreciate the true conditions and they had a tendency to repeat the same mistakes; for example, Haig repeated the Somme at Passchendaele and was totally unaware of the waterlogged ground there.

In 1915 the Germans tried to defeat the Russians. They came close to success as the Tsarist troops were thrown back 480 kilometres at the expense of two million casualties; however, Russia would not surrender, the Germans ran out of steam and the war went on. In fact in 1916 the Russians launched a successful counter-attack against the Austrians – reflecting the pattern that had emerged from the beginning on the Eastern Front: the Russians could defeat the Austrians but not the Germans and the Germans constantly needed to come to the Austrians' aid. Indeed from 1915 the Austrians ceased to operate as an independent army; they now also had a southern front as Italy joined the Allied side (May 1915) though it failed to make much impact. Turkey had already joined the Central Powers' side (November 1914) and had resisted successfully an Allied attack on Gallipoli (1915). The Central Powers defeated the Serbs in 1915 and went on to beat the Rumanians in 1916.

The stalemate on the Western Front left the Germans in charge of most of Belgium and a large part of north-eastern France. Therefore the onus was on the Allies to drive the Germans out; the latter just had to sit tight – which is largely what they did (Verdun being a costly exception in 1916). Allied offensives in 1915, 1916 (the Somme) and 1917 (Nivelle and Passchendaele) failed to make a breakthrough, though the Germans did shorten the line in 1917 (by which time they were considerably outnumbered – 2.5 million soldiers facing 3.9 million).

The year 1917 was in many ways a crucial year. The Russian war effort collapsed; the Tsar was removed in March and the Bolsheviks came to power in November, in effect eliminating Russia from the war. This was a terrible blow to the Allies but was more than compensated for by the intervention of the United States (April), brought in by a combination of unrestricted submarine warfare, German intrigues in Mexico and considerations of economic and political affiliation.

However, the entry of the Americans into the war did not make an immediate difference and the end of the war in the East gave Germany a second chance. Just as the collapse of Russia gave Germany the incentive to carry on, the entry of the USA did likewise for the Allies.

Quite why the war had gone on this long also had a lot to do with the resolve of the powers to support each other to the end – what brought them into the war in the first place continued to be valid reasons for going on; no one on the Allied side wanted to see a Europe dominated by Germany. Similarly on the German side, surrender would mean the end of Germany as a great power, and the war had been fought precisely in order not only to maintain Germany's great power status but to enhance it. Moreover, it is worth stating that what is also remarkable is the enormous sacrifice ordinary people of all sides were prepared to make in a cause they felt to be just. Accordingly, given the political resolve on the part of both governments and people, nations committed all their resources to the war effort.

This was the first total war, in which governments extended their control over all aspects of life (manpower, food supplies, industrial and agricultural production) and sustained morale by propaganda – exaggerating successes, concealing setbacks, building up heroes, and condemning the enemies' barbarity.

Why was there no negotiated settlement?

The basic problem was that the Germans considered themselves partially victorious and were reluctant to give up Belgium. In addition, their annexationist aims, brought to fruition in the East with the Treaty of Brest Litovsk in March 1918, made negotiations impractical. Moreover, intransigence was not confined to the Germans – no government wanted to restore a balance of power. Each side wanted a lasting peace and felt that this could only be achieved by total victory; the enemy must be defeated for all time – it was to be 'a war to end all wars'. In any event, the enormous sacrifices that had been made in terms of loss of life made a compromise seem unworthy.

Nevertheless, by 1917 cracks were beginning to appear in the resolution of the belligerents – Russia collapsed, the French army was incapacitated by widespread mutiny (but the Germans did not notice!), a majority in the Reichstag (German parliament) called for peace, and President Wilson of the USA called for a peace settlement based on his famous 14 points. However, Wilson's talk of self-determination and democracy did not exactly strike a chord with the decision-makers in Vienna and Berlin. In addition, the new Austro-Hungarian Emperor, Karl I, made serious but unsuccessful attempts to negotiate, and the Pope made an appeal for peace on the basis of a return of the *status quo ante bellum* (i.e. the position of 1914). No one was listening and the war went on. The generals, the politicians and even the majority of the people (as far as we can tell) seemed stoically resolved to stick it out in the belief that ultimate victory would be achieved. From the Germans' point of view, victory on the Eastern Front had presented them with another opportunity to attempt a decisive offensive in the West.

Why did Germany fail in 1918?

Because the Germans had been so greedy at Brest Litovsk, Paul von Hindenburg and Erich von Ludendorff (in charge since 1916) had been forced to leave a million men behind in the East. Ludendorff was only able to transfer 52 divisions to the West (less than a million men) and was still without the numerical superiority that was needed to ensure a breakthrough.

Yet between 21 March and mid-July the Germans made considerable headway, advancing 65 kilometres around the Somme and 55 kilometres in the South to the Marne – advances not seen since 1914 (see Figure 6 on page 108). However, Ludendorff did not appear to have clear objectives and failed to confound Allied reserves by moving his attack around; there was no breakthrough – the Allied line held (in this

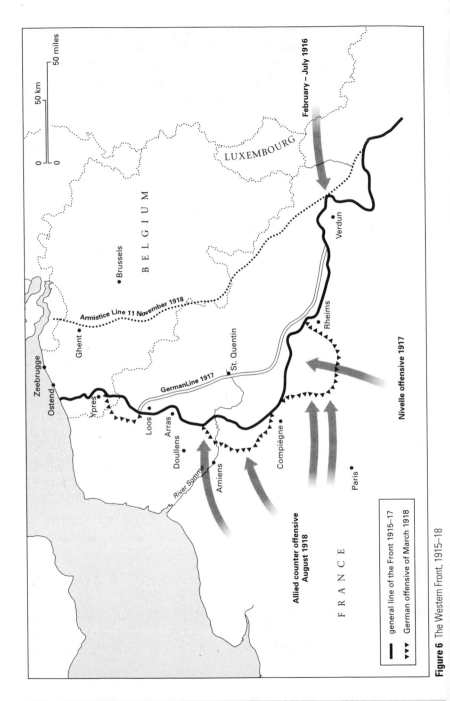

Figure 6 The Western Front, 1915–18

extremity the British had accepted overall French command) and the Germans found themselves trying to hold a much longer line with much fewer men. In fact by the summer, the Germans had lost about a million men and were back to about 2.5 million, whereas the Allies had gained about a million Americans. The game was up; Ludendorff's gamble had failed.

The Allies struck back using planes and tanks, hitting the Germans in a number of different places, then breaking off and resuming elsewhere. At no stage did the Germans have time to draw breath and send in their reserves. In fact, fully one-third of the German army spent its time travelling by train from one sector to another. By the end of August, the Germans had been forced back to their spring line. The Allied advance continued throughout September and October pushing the Germans from most of their French conquests, but not from the greater part of Belgium and not yet into Germany (except for a small area in Alsace). Indeed the German line held and the Allies were making firm dispositions for 1919 and even talking of 1920.

When the end came in November 1918, it was very sudden and unexpected. The surrender of Bulgaria at the end of September and the capitulation of Turkey and Austria in October/early November deprived Germany of allies but were not the reasons for Germany's defeat – after all, Germany had been sustaining its allies throughout. Defeat came not from the battle front nor from the home front, but from the very people who had started the war in the first place, the generals of the High Command. Ludendorff had completely lost his nerve by the end of September and on 1 October stated that he anticipated a catastrophic defeat and urged the Kaiser to 'request an armistice without any hesitation', only a 'quick end' could save the army from destruction.

When the German government asked for an armistice on 3 October (in the belief that President Wilson of the USA would grant a soft peace), it came as a complete shock to the German people as the true position had been concealed from them. For many, victory had suddenly turned into an inexplicable defeat. The Germans who had stoically borne shortages created by the British blockade now lost heart and the home front crumbled. Naval mutiny at the end of the month led to revolution and the collapse of internal order by early November. The Kaiser was forced to abdicate and Germany signed an armistice on 11 November. The war was finally at an end.

Conclusion

What the generals did not appreciate was that the alliances had created a remarkable balance of power in 1914: no single power had sufficient superiority for decisive victory in the short term. There is no doubt that Germany could have beaten France on a one-to-one basis, just as Russia could have beaten Austria, but 1914 was not to be a rerun of 1870. Similarly, during the war Austria could not have kept going after the defeats of 1916 (or even those of 1914), France would have collapsed in 1917 after the disastrous Nivelle offensive and the mutinies, and Italy would have done the same after Caporetto, had not each of them received support from its allies. The alliance system virtually guaranteed that the war would not be decided quickly.

It is interesting to note that the one ally that did collapse, Russia, was strategically isolated and could not be bailed out by its allies. Once the war became one of attrition, numbers and resources would count; and the Central Powers did not have the numbers and the resources. 'A calculation of manufacturing production in 1913 showed Germany and Austria together as having 19.2 per cent of total world production, while France, Russia and Britain together had 27.9 per cent' (Philip Bell, from Paul Hayes (ed.), *Themes in Modern European History 1890–1945*, Routledge, 1992), though it should be noted that it was Great Britain that really made the difference (as indeed the United States did later).

In August 1914 the *Entente* powers put 202 divisions into the field to the Central Powers' 143. Two years later the figure was 405 to 369. In numerical terms the Allied powers held the advantage throughout with perhaps the exception of the beginning of 1918. A glance at the figures below shows that the Allies mobilised something like

40 million men during the course of the war, whereas the Central Powers could only manage about 25 million.

Given these odds, it is remarkable that Germany had such military success and held out for so long. Clearly its central position and efficient use of manpower and resources counted for a great deal, as did the fact that Allied economic superiority could not be brought to bear instantly – but the fact remains that once it was (by 1918), the Central Powers could not really win. Accordingly, they did suffer defeat and a complete breakdown of their economic and political structures; it was the price they paid for starting the war.

War expenditure and mobilised forces

Country	Armed forces 1914 (millions)	Total mobilised (millions)	Expenditure (billions of dollars)
British Empire	1	9.5	23
France	4	8.2	9.3
Russia	5.9	13	5.4
Italy	1.25 (1915)	5.6	3.2
USA	—	3.8	17.1
Total	12.15	40.1	58
Germany	4.5	13.25	19.9
Austria-Hungary	3	9.0	4.7
Turkey	2	2.85	0.1
Total	9.5	25.1	24.7

FURTHER READING

This is a short, selective bibliography. Many of the books cited have extensive bibliographies.

There are a number of short works on the origins of the First World War (like this one), but these have not been included as after reading one short work you should be looking for depth of knowledge rather than more of the same.

The wider context

Good surveys of international relations in the nineteenth century are:

F. R. Bridge and Roger Bullen *The Great Powers and the European States System 1815–1914* (Addison Wesley Longman, 1980)

C. J. Bartlett *Peace, War and the European Powers 1814–1914* (Macmillan, 1996) – the most recent survey

Paul Kennedy *The Rise and Fall of the Great Powers* (Unwin Hyman, 1988) – this covers a lot more than just the nineteenth century.

Collections of essays

The Coming of the First World War edited by R. J. W. Evans and Hartmut Pogge von Strandmann (OUP, 1988)

Decisions for War, 1914 edited by Keith Wilson (UCL Press, 1995) – the most recent compilation – very useful.

Individual countries

S. R. Williamson *Austria-Hungary and the Origins of the First World War* (Macmillan, 1991)

Z. S. Steiner *Britain and the Origins of the First World War* (Macmillan, 1977)

J. F. V. Keiger *France and the Origins of the First World War* (Macmillan, 1983)

V. R. Berghahn *Germany and the Approach of War in 1914*, 2nd edition (Macmillan, 1993)

D. C. B. Lieven *Russia and the Origins of the First World War* (Macmillan, 1983).

The war

Correlli Barnett *The Great War* (Park Lane Press, 1979) – for the coffee table

Keith Robbins *The First World War* (OUP, 1984) – short, but good

Martin Gilbert *First World War* (Weidenfeld and Nicolson, 1994) – but see Hew Strachan's trenchant criticisms in the *TLS* (16.9.94)

Holger H. Herwig *The First World War – Germany and Austria-Hungary 1914–1918* (Arnold, 1997) – very good.

INDEX

Longman History in Depth

Series editor: Christopher Culpin

Titles in the series

Hitler and Nazism (0 582 29736 2)

Causes of the Second World War (0 582 29650 1)

Stalin and the Soviet Union (0 582 29733 8)

Origins of the First World War (0 582 29522 X)

The Russian Revolution (0 582 29731 1)

Parnell and the Irish Question (0 582 29628 5)

Gladstone (0 582 29521 1)

Chartism (0 582 29735 4)

Oliver Cromwell (0 582 29734 6)

Charles I (0 582 29732 X)

Henry VII (0 582 29691 9)

Pearson Education Limited,
Edinburgh Gate, Harlow,
Essex, CM20 2JE, England
and Associated Companies throughout the world.

The right of Graham Darby to the identified as the author of this Work has
been asserted by him in accordance with the Copyright, Designs and Patents
Act of 1988.

First published 1998
Fourth impression 2003
© Addison Wesley Longman Limited 1998

Set in 9.5/13pt Stone Serif
Printed in Singapore (FOP)

ISBN 0 582 29522 X

Acknowledgements

We are grateful to the following for permission to reproduce photographs:

Mary Evans Picture Library, page 20 top; Hulton Deutsch Collection, page 64;
Popperfoto, pages 19, 20 centre and bottom.

We were unable to trace the copyright holder of the following and would be
grateful for any information that would enable us to do so, page 52.

Cover photograph: the Kaiser instructing a group of Generals during the last
military manoeuvres before the outbreak of war in 1914. Popperfoto

We are grateful to EDEXCEL Foundation, London Examinations for
permission to reproduce extracts and questions from 'European Diplomacy
1905–1907' and 'The Agadir Crisis 1911–1913' in London GCE A' Level paper
1995, pages 18–19, 20–21, and 'German Military Planning' in London GCE A'
Level paper 1996, pages 20, 21.

The publisher's policy is to use paper manufactured from sustainable forests.